American Premi
To
JUKEBOXES
and
SLOT MACHINES
GUMBALLS - TRADE STIMULATORS - ARCADE

by
Jerry Ayliffe

BOOKS AMERICANA
INC

ISBN 0-89689-055-4

i

TABLE OF CONTENTS

ACKNOWLEDGEMENTS

I would like to thank the following people in the field of coin-operated machines for sharing their knowledge, and allowing me to photograph their machines: Bruce J. Benjamin, Al Breuner, Steve Brooks, Bill Butterfield, Tom Cockrill, Jack and Michael Connolly, Jerry Cordy, Phil Cunningham, Jim and Susan Davy, Marsh Fey, Dick Graves, Steve Gronowski, Larry Johnson, Marshall Larks, Rick Lee, Larry Lubliner, John McWayne, Bud Meyer, Allan Pall, Neil Rasmussen, Fredrick Roth, Mr. Russell, Alan Sax, Gary Taplin, Bill and Norene Ward, Wayne and Hilda Warren, Bill and Carol Whelan, and D.R. Williams.

These people were all very open and helpful in answering my questions and allowing me to photograph their machines. I would like to single out the following people who extensively shared their expertise. I also appreciate the fact that they allowed me to spread photographic paraphernalia all over their homes and shops to photograph their machines. Thanks again, Steve Brooks, Bill Butterfield, Tom Cockrill, Phil Cunningham, John McWayne, and Bill and Carol Whelan. I sincerely hope that I haven't left anyone out.

ACKNOWLEDGMENTS

INTRODUCTION

It's very gratifying to see the interest in our first book on coin-operated machines. The number of books sold can only verify the fact that the interest in this hobby has grown dramatically.

The purpose of the second book, as was the first, is to give people an informative look at coin-operated antiques. Many listings and photographs have been added to this edition. It would be next to impossible to list every coin-operated machine that was ever made. However, a genuine attempt has been made to give the most comprehensive list available.

Pricing is a very difficult area. Dealers like to see prices on the high side, while buyers like to see things on the low side. That is, until the machine is in their collection, and then the high side is better. In one case that I know of, an insurance claim for $9,000 was settled based on values listed in the first book. For this possibility alone, it is important not to quote unrealistically low prices. Regionality is also important. A Wurlitzer 1015 might sell for $7,000 in Beverly Hills. Transporting the same machine to Dubuque would make a selling price more like $4,500. Please keep in mind the prices listed reflect the opinion of the author based on personal buying and selling experience, prices at auction, and advertised prices in various publications. The prices lean toward the retail side, and in order to make a profit, dealers will expect to pay less. One last statement on pricing; there was a lot of praise from very respected people in this hobby, and some grumbles concerning prices in the first book. All in all, from the feedback I received, the prices in the first edition seemed to pretty well hit the mark.

This book concerns itself only with machines produced for the American market. This is not to say that export machines have no value. However, the interest in this field of collecting is mostly centered around domestic machines.

As a service to the reader, a number of tabloids, periodicals, books, publishers, and dealers related to the hobby have been listed. This is not intended to be a blanket endorsement of those listings; the intention, rather, is to inform the reader, and give as much help as possible.

With regard to dates, dates listed are the first year of manufacture, or the first patent date. Realize that some machines didn't reach the market for several years after the first patent date. Also some machines were changed several times during a production run of many years, and the model shown may not be the first one produced. Where less certainty concerning dates exists, the year is marked "circa".

After the release of the first edition, a number of people took the time to call or write the publisher, and get my phone number. I appreciated hearing from these people, and I'll make it a little easier by giving my phone number this time, which is (916) 933-0952. Mornings before noon (California time) and evenings between 7:00 p.m. and 10:00 p.m. are the best times to call. I'll look forward to hearing from you, and I hope you enjoy the book.

I. Are coin-operated collectibles a good investment?

A fairly well agreed upon axiom for intrinsic value is supply and demand. When demand is high, and supply is low, the price of an object rises.

Coin-operated machines are a supreme example of American marketing genius. They were the clerk that never needed a holiday, was always on the job on time, was never sick (well, almost never), and never asked for overtime pay. In order to make up for the lack of the human touch, manufacturers made the machines attractive and gay. Some of the machines were even animated to give them a human quality. The result, of course, was a great success. Our legacy is some of the most beautiful and unique works of art our nation has ever produced.

Works of art? Undoubtedly some members of the art community will be in a snit over that comment. But think about the beauty represented in an upright slot machine, for example, or a beautiful Wurlitzer jukebox from the 1940's. They are beautiful to look at, and beyond that, they performed amazing mechanical feats. To me that's a lot more like art than some modern paintings I have seen.

Unfortunately, at the time they were in use they weren't thought of as works of art. Once they had performed their function, which was to make money, they weren't much good for anything. So they were often thrown away. Manufacturers were in the business of selling machines. The best way to sell machines was to produce a new, improved model. They encouraged operators to trade in their old machines, and the manufacturers and distributors, for very practical reasons, shipped last year's model to the dump. The automobile industry's approach to marketing is very similar, and that's why old cars are also very scarce.

That establishes the supply side of our economic equation. The question is, how much supply is there? That's the part that no one really knows for sure. We see many more slots on the market than there were three years ago. Of course, there has been a great deal of publicity concerning slot machines. This coupled with dramatic increases in prices, seemed to bring a number of machines out of the woodwork. Does that mean that there are a lot more machines hidden away? No one know for sure. My personal opinion is that 70% of the slot machines that are out there have already been found. The remaining 30% will be much slower to come to the surface than the first 70%. Remember, this is just my speculative opinion, and I could be completely wrong.

What does this have to do with the demand side of the equation? At least in the case of the slot machines, there seems to be a temporary over supply which has caused prices on the market to stabilize.

How does this relate to jukeboxes, trade stimulators, vending machines, and arcade items? While they haven't received as much publicity as slot machines, their position in the marketplace seems to follow a path parallel to that of the slot machines; much as silver prices follow gold prices.

Some collectors will scoff at this economic discussion. After all, on a higher plane we collect these machines for their unique beauty, not to make money; or is it both? The people that already have large collections, that were purchased for much lower prices than the current market have somewhat less concern for what's happening with the economics of collecting. They are in a more or less no lose position, except when they try to add to their collections.

The concern here is more with the new collector who is just starting out, or maybe just the person who would like to own one slot machine for his game room. With prices for the better machines in the $2,000 plus range, for most people buying one slot machine would be a major investment. The question is, is it a wise investment?

It has already been established by the marketplace that coin-operated collectibles are valuable, in varying degrees, of course, depending on the desirability and rarity of the machine. The questions that are being asked are will they hold their value? Will they increase at a faster or slower rate, and to what level, as compared to other investments?

The following is my philosophy which is based on my own personal opinion. I value this opinion very much, however it is not meant to be advice to the reader, so please don't take it as such. Here goes . . . To me, the uniqueness and beauty of the coin-operated collectibles will never be truly duplicated. I believe that the current over-supply of slot machines is a temporary situation. During periods of recession, people like to have money available for emergencies; understandably so. However, economic downturns are eventually followed by economic upturns. When inflation reasserts itself hard goods, such as collectibles, should go up in value. Past economic history has been that during periods of heavy inflation, consumers rush to buy hard goods. Since I enjoy having these machines in my home, I have what I feel is an excellent situation. I have an investment that I receive great pleasure from. Most economists advise diversity of investment, and I agree with that philosophy. Also, I invest in machines mostly because I want to own that piece enough to pay the price that is being asked. Although for me there is always an eye to future value, I realize that with any investment there is an element of risk.

Are coin-operated collectibles a good investment? No one really knows for sure. Ultimately, that's a question everyone has to answer for himself. Personally, I'm betting my chips that they are.

II. Where Can I Find The Best Deal?

In the first edition there was a section on where to find coin-operated machines, and it proved to be helpful to a number of people. For the sake of review, and for new readers, here is an outline of that information with some additions. As we go along there will be comments as to the potential and means for good deals in each area.

(1) Specialty antique dealers: With the popularity of the coin-op hobby, more and more antique dealers are targeting in on this area. Often the prices are high at these specialized stores, but there are some good deals to be had. It is important to remember that these people locate, repair, and, in some cases, stand behind their

merchandise. Finding a dealer that is trustworthy can be extremely important. After a good relationship has been developed with a dealer, he can often offer good advice on potential purchases from other sources. If the dealer has a repair facility, and most do, this can be extremely valuable when a machine breaks down. Another important function is as a trading post. Most people who get involved with coin-operated machines find out it is like a disease, however it is a friendly disease that is usually not harmful. One symptom is that after the purchase of one machine, the buyer is certain to want another and another. Some people get Tradeitis. That's where the victim constantly wants to trade up, seeking machines that are rarer and more majestic than the ones they already possess. This is where an understanding dealer can be helpful in facilitating such trades. Take your dealer out to lunch; be nice to him. He can be very helpful to your quest.

(2) Coin-operated shows: several years ago the only show featuring machines was the "Loose Change" Fun Fair. This show has always been an amazing display of drop-coin antiques. However, for some people in the East, the trip to California was just too far. In 1981 shows seemed to pop up everywhere. Denver, Houston, and Chicago were just a few of the cities hosting shows of this sort. The best way to keep abreast of these shows is to subscribe to "Coin Slot" or "Loose Change", which is listed in the information section in the back of the book.

For the most part, these shows are like a smorgasbord for the collector. Because there is a great selection, the competition is usually pretty good. This tends to keep prices at very reasonable levels. By the amount of buying being done by dealers at the 1981 "Loose Change" show, it was evident that prices were pretty good for those who knew what to look for.

To me, the best way to view a show is to make a quick pass, and note potential good buys. Then a second pass, much more concentrated, is for serious consideration of purchases. Obviously, if I see something that I really want that is a good buy the first time through, I buy it.

Shows are one of the best places to buy machines at a fair price. Just be careful and take your time.

(3) Auctions: The potential for good deals at auctions is roughly equal to the potential for bad deals. Previewing the merchandise is absolutely essential. Don't be afraid to open the back door and

look at the mechanism. Look everywhere you can think of for the hint of something that is not right. Not to overstate the case, many machines are sold at auction that are very good, and in some cases they go for very low prices. Remember, however, auctions are also dumping grounds for machines that are not up to par. I would almost always rather buy a machine that is in orignial condition at an auction. Restored machines are sometimes incomplete machines that are quickly put together with unoriginal parts.

The best way to find out about upcoming auctions is to subscribe to "The Antique Trader" or "Coin Slot', which are listed in the back of the book in the information section. The chances for a good buy at an auction is great, just be careful.

(4) Antique Publications: There are a number of publications that have classified ads with Coin-operated machines for sale. Several of these are: "The Antique Trader", "Coin Slot Magazine", "Jukebox Trader", and "Loose Change". Information on all of these sources is listed in the back of this book.

Several years ago this source was one of the few good ones for finding machines. Now, however, with the emergence of many specialty dealers, auctions, and shows that feature coin-op the importance of this area has dwindled, but it still is a good marketplace and sometimes offers exceptional deals. Please pay attention to the safeguards that were mentioned in the first edition regarding buying long distance. It can sometimes be very hazardous sending money for merchandise that is sight unseen.

(5) General antique dealers: As mentioned earlier, dealers who specialize in coin-operated antiques are a fairly new occurence. In the old days general antique dealers were the only ones to market these oddities. Quite often, these dealers had very little knowledge and the demand was low, creating correspondingly low prices.

This is a fairly rare occurence now. Most antique dealers have become very educated on the value of machines. However, dealers sometimes fall into good deals, and they will pass these on to their buyers. The best advice is to establish yourself with several dealers. Pick ones with whom you have rapport, and stop in and see them on a regular basis. It's important to treat them fairly in order to get the same consideration back. Buying something once in awhile doesn't hurt either.

(6) Local newspaper classified ads: The place most people overlook is newspaper classifieds. True, the pages will not be filled

with coin-operated machines, however, from time to time a classic good deal will come up. One thing that is extremely important in this endeavor is to find out as much information on the phone as possible. It's amazing how many wild goose chases occur because the machine was not represented clearly over the telephone. One other thing seems to be prevalent with private party sales. A high percentage of the public has been educated to the fact that coin-operated machines are valuable. Often a machine can be priced higher than it would be available for from a reputable dealer. So beware: That hidden gold often turns out to be pyrite.

(7) Flea Markets: Flea Markets are probably the last frontier for good deals. Recently a friend picked up an upright slot mechanism, and later, a cabinet for under $500. Admittedly, there will be a lot of work in restoration. The nice part is that when it's completed, it will be worth at least $8,500. That's not bad for a day's work. The key is that this fellow goes consistantly, week after week to the flea markets, and the good finds are few and far between.

Addicted flea market people agree that the key to success is going early, and consistently. The people who are committed to this philosophy seem to find at least two or more really good deals a year, with some other decent finds in the bargain.

(8) Word of Mouth: Last but not least is word of mouth. This is one of the most exciting areas because great finds seem to turn up in the most unlikely places sometimes. Word of mouth simply means talking about your interests at every available opportunity.

When I'm in other people's houses and I see any antiques at all, even one single item, a little light goes on. People like to talk about their possessions, and an inquiry about their antiques will generally be welcomed, and greatly appreciated. I enjoy all antiques, so I generally am very interested to hear what the people have to say about their prizes. If the opportunity arises, and it generally does, I mention that I'm interested in antique coin-operated machines, such as slot machines. This elicits some interesting responses, usually very positive. It's amazing how many good finds either directly or indirectly have turned up due to these conversations.

Another good idea is to have business cards printed up. This is the one I use:

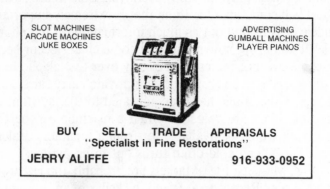
This was mentioned in the first edition, and it bears repeating. Business cards will do no good unless they are passed out. I know of several cases where a $10 investment in business cards rewarded the investors with four figure dollar returns. The whole key was that these people passed their cards out, and talked about their hobby at every possible opportunity. This is also a great way to stumble onto people who have valuable restoration skills. Collecting other people's cards, and keeping them on files can be an equally important exercise.

Coin-operated shows, auctions, flea markets, garage sales, and antique stores are other places that are great to pass out and collect cards. It all boils down to establishing, and belonging to a network of friends and associates that are interested in our hobby.

III. Some Pitfalls To Watch Out For

One of the most irritating things that is happening in our hobby is the disguised sale of reproduction machines.

Reproduction machines very simply are completely new machines that are counterfeits of original machines. Even if these machines are represented as what they are by the original producers, as they work their way through different hands they often get misrepresented. Just like counterfeit money, some unsuspecting person often ends up with a turkey. For this reason, and it's unfortunate, a buyer has to be very suspect of machines that are in mint restored condition. Some restorers are bead-blasting mechs, deep sanding cabinets, and polishing and replating all metal parts. Technically if done right this could be considered to be a fine restoration. However, to an inexperienced buyer a mint restored machine and a reproduction can look very much alike. My advice is to look for signs of originality, such as hairline cracks in the casting, dents or age spots in the wood, slightly rusted parts, and aged award cards. Probably the best advice is to buy a machine in good, unrestored condition, and have it restored by a reputable person.

A problem that is related to the first involves machines that have been put together with some original parts and some reproduction parts. Often these machines are much harder to identify than reproduced machines, since some of the age character comes through in the original parts. These machines usually come on the market in restored condition. Once again, with bead-blasted mechs, polished, replated, and highly refinished cabinets. In these cases the machines are thoroughly restored to disguise and blend the old and new parts. The advice in this case is once again, to buy a machine in good, original condition. It is unfortunate to give this advice, in a way. Many reputable dealers go to a good deal of expense to put machines in a restored condition. Almost everyone enjoys a machine more that has been restored to its original splendor. Also, there are many more examples of machines that are found in terrible condition with some parts missing. It would be horrible to throw these machines in the junkpile, and it's often hard to sell them as is, so the logical solution is restoration. As mentioned earlier in the book, that's one reason why it's very important to deal with someone that is trustworthy.

Beware of mysterious, one of a kind machines. That's not to say pass up anything you haven't heard of, or seen before. Just be careful, and look for phoniness, or an amateur look to a machines. This can be difficult, because some of the rarest machines were produced by small shops with unsophisticated tooling. For example, some of the much-coveted Fey machines have a very primitive look. On the other hand, I have seen homemade contraptions that are little more than junk sell for some fairly high prices.

To me, information and experience are the biggest safeguards to avoiding bad buys. I personally subscribe to all of the publications, and own all of the books listed in the back of this book. These printed items are a constant source of reference and help to me. If I anticipate buying a machine, I try to locate a photo of it in one of my reference sources. Neither am I bashful about taking the book with me, and comparing the photo to the actual machine offered for sale. Realize that because it's in print, it isn't necessarily the gospel. This is a relatively new field of interest. Much of the information is folklore passed from one person to the next. Inaccuracies are never intentional, but some are inevitable when putting a large body of information together. All things considered, these books and periodicals are still very valuable.

One last tidbit: Don't be afraid to ask questions. A great philosopher once said that there's no such thing as a dumb question. I try to listen more than I talk. It's a scientific fact that you are not learning one single thing while you are talking. That's not to say that sharing information is not an important thing to do. However, I sometimes see people who are trying to be such bigshots and know-it-alls that they don't have time to learn anything.

IV. More thoughts about repair and restoration

In the first book I encouraged people to restore their own machines. My thoughts really haven't changed on that subject. There is great pleasure in restoring a machine to its original beauty if it's done right. Savings are also generally better if machines are purchased in good, restorable condition. Best of all, it lets the buyers know exactly what he has, and what he ends up with.

By way of explanation, if a buyer picks up a machine that is a mass of parts lying here and there in a box, well, then, at least he knows what the starting point was. He isn't buying a totally restored machine with no idea as to which parts are original, or which ones are recast. On the other hand, a poor, amateurish restoration is worse than no restoration at all. If you aren't inclined toward perfection in your work, it might be better to find a professional who can do it right.

Now comes the tough part; what constitutes a good restoration? And, even harder than the first question, which machines should be restored, and which ones should be left as is? There is a groundswell amongst many of the collectors that shows a strong preference for unrestored machines in good original condition. Machines like these have always been the dream of the true coin-op enthusiast. However, with lower availability they are in stronger demand than ever. It makes me cringe to see machines that are in nice original condition arbitrarily restored because it makes them more saleable, or because they look prettier that way. This decision, of course, rests in the hands of the person who owns the machine. This sort of reminds me of a few millionaires who moved into Beverly Hills and put plastic flowers and plants out in front for easy maintenance. I guess if you have the dough you can do anything you want. It's just a shame that these great treasures will be passed on for posterity looking like something that belongs in a custom car show.

That brings up the next point: Once a machine has been judged to be in bad enough condition to need a restoration, what is the right way to restore it? This is the area that probably just about everyone has some disagreement on. Well, here goes my opinion on the subject. First of all, if a machine is going to be restored, it should be totally disassembled (possibly excluding the mech if it's in good working condition and free of rust). Outer aluminum parts should be buffed. This will produce a higher luster than when they come from the factory but it will become duller in a matter of months. Outer cast iron castings and other metals should be plated or painted in a finish as close to factory as possible. Sometimes there's a choice, such as the Mills Check Boy that comes in either a nickle, or an oxidized copper finish, according to original factory literature. Exterior metal painting and wood finishing should be as close to original finish as factory. There is some argument on colors, since manufacturers would paint with various colors on special order. This seemingly gives license to people to paint slot machines in colors that match their decorating scheme. It's hard to believe, but I have seen so-called expert restorations where slot machine fronts were painted with automotive candy apple green. I like to see the colors as close to the original designer's intention as possible.

Wood finishing is another area that deserves a few words. Thank goodness for polyurethane; it really works great on wood that is exposed to the weather. However, seeing it in deep glossy layers on the side of a glorious machine makes my eyes water. Here I have to admit to a sin. My tendency is to use lacquer in almost all cases, where in fact original factory finishes were often varnishes or shellac. I guess the practical side of me wins over the purist. Lacquer is fast, goes on dust free, and gives a rich finish that closely resembles the original. In truth, the best restoration would be one with the original finish.

Inner mechanism pieces that are rusted should be wire brushed

11

or bead blasted. This process will usually remove the original plating, so they should be replated or shot with a clear rust inhibitor. The mechanism needs to be adjusted to perfect working order, and lubricated at wear points.

When the machine is reassembled, the restoration is first rate (in my opinion) if the machine looks like it did the day it rolled off the assembly line.

What kind of collection is the best?

Unfortunately, in the process of collecting just about anything, the chance of bumping into some balloon bursters is tremendous. Especially when a person first starts out in a hobby, there will always be people who own more desirable items. A high percentage of the people who are involved in coin-operated machines are really great people. However, there is a small percentage that can't wait to tell you how great their stuff is, and how crummy yours is. That seems to be true of life in general; however, it's particularly intense in the endeavor of collecting. What's the problem with this? Mainly, it's discouraging. I think many people who would really enjoy this hobby give up because they feel they will never be able to have a "nice collection". Here's an example of a conversation I overheard at a show. Mr. New Collector had just picked up a Groetchen Pok-O-Reel trade stimulator. To digress for a minute, for those who are not familiar with that machine, it's a small 5 reel poker game from the 1940's, and it's not a rare, or extremely expensive machine. Mr. New Collector was proudly carrying his new find along with him, when he had the misfortune of standing next to Mr. Ugly Collector. Mr. Ugly Collector turned around and asked Mr. New Collector where he found that piece of junk. We can all talk about having a thick skin, but those kinds of comments are bound to effect us more than we would like to admit.

What am I trying to say here? Just that we are involved in preserving one of the most interesting phenomenons in our country's history. All of the machines from the easiest to find, to the hardest ones to find are exciting and fun to have in our surroundings. In fact, I envy the new collector; almost everything he finds is fresh and exciting to him. Hunting for machines is an adventure that loses its glamour when it's turned into an ego trip.

What kind of collection is the best? That's easy. It's made up of the things that you enjoy the most that are within your reach.

For instance, I think it would be fun to have just one of each of the different types of trade stimulators. For example, I would like one 3 reeler, one poker game, one roulette, and so forth, to illustrate the interesting variety of games that were available in trade stiumlators. This type of collection wouldn't cost a fortune, and it would really be fun to show guests who have probably not even heard of trade stimulators. It might be nice to have one item from each area of coin-operated. That is, a trade stimulator, a slot machine, a vendor, and an arcade piece. It would sure liven up a family room. I have added these things to my own family room, and it's amazing what a good feeling it gives me and my family to be in that room. That's where the true joy of collecting comes from; not from trying to play one-upmanship with another collector.

VI. Slot Machines

Slot machines are essentially any machine with a coin slot that involves gambling or speculation. The term "slot machine" is being used because it seems to be the most accepted terminology for coin-operated gambling devices. One arm bandits, bell machines, 3 reelers, uprights, and trade stimulators are all jargon for various machines that fall under the general heading of slot machines. In fact, slot machines in the early days meant anything that was operated with a coin. This section of the book will deal more specifically with automatic payout type gambling devices. This primarily includes the early upright wheel of fortune type machines, and the 3 reelers that are most familiar. There are various other oddities that do not fall into any specific group. These machines which are the automatic payout type, but are not in the upright or three-reeler category are also included in this section.

Slot machines began their predominant history in the 1890's, although there were earlier examples of gambling devices. The most popular machines of that period were the large upright slots with one disk that resembled a wheel of fortune. The player selected a color category or several colors, placed his bet in the appropriate color coded slots, and gave the wheel a spin. If the wheel landed on the selected color, there was an automatic payout.

Automatic payout is an important concept. What was so attractive about automatic payout? First and foremost it gave the storekeeper, saloon owner, restaurant owner or whomever an automatic employee. While the businessman was taking care of business, this machine automatically took the customer's money, entertained him, and paid him if he was a winner in the transaction. This was an employee that was never late for work, was willing to do its job, never needed instruction, and didn't collect an hourly wage.

These upright slot machines were popular with customers as a source of entertainment that enticed the underlying human interest in risk. The businessman liked them because they were a source of revenue. Slot machine manufacturers did their best to fill that need. In the spirit of bigger and better, there were double and triple models. Some even had music boxes that further entertained the customer while he gambled, and circumvented gambling laws.

In 1905 a San Francisco inventor named Charles Fey revolutionized the slot machine industry. Charles Fey produced the first counter top, 3 reel, payout type slot machine and named it the Liberty Bell. Why did this machine become so popular? For one thing, it was alot more exciting to watch and to play. There were bigger payoffs and more winning combinations available. The machines were also compact, easy to set on a bar top, a store counter, or a multitude of other locations. The rest is history. Literally millions of machines have been produced using essentially the same foremat.

Mills was quick to copy the Liberty Bell with their Operator's Bell. Caille and Watling later followed with similar copies and in the 1920's a host of other manufacturers jumped on the bandwagon.

With the advent of all these machines the law and order types felt obliged to stamp them out. Laws were brought about to stop gambling machines, but the manufacturers and operators were not about to give up this highly lucrative venture. What they did instead was to make their machines hide under the guise being of vending machines. They did this by hanging a confection vendor on the side of the machine or incorporating it on the front. Every time a customer inserted a coin, he had the option of recieving a package of gum or candy. Also if the customer hit a payout, the machine dropped tokens, instead of money. Therefore if the operator wished to exchange the player's token for merchandise, or cash, that was strictly up to him.

Slot machines hit their heyday in the depression. Law enforcement seemed to turn its head and 3 reelers began appearing everywhere. It would seem that during an economic disaster, gambling would be the last thing on people's minds. Human nature, however, turned out to be the reverse. Maybe people felt that gambling was their only chance at beating the system.

During and after this period, the operators became more and more corrupt, and our government took a more active role in enforcing the morality of our country. In 1951 the federal government passed a law prohibiting the transportation of slot machines across state lines. This coupled with stricter enforcement of gambling laws by many states put an end to the 3 reeler's heyday. Nevada and New Jersey now are the only states that allow slot machine gambling.

Where does all of this leave the individual that would like to have a slot machine in his home? Unfortunately, for many years this individual was considered to be a criminal. In 1976 after a great deal of lobbying, the California legislature consented to private ownership of slot machines if the machine was made prior to 1941. Since then, many states have followed suit.

It is generally agreed upon by collectors that they don't own their machines for the purpose of gambling. They want these machines for the memory of our past, because they are works of art in their own sense, and they're just plain fun.

SLOT MACHINE INDEX

ILLUS. PAGE NO.	MACHINE NAME	PRICE RANGE
—	Caille Victor Floor Wheel 1902	$8000-15,000
—	Caille Bullfrog Floor Machine 1903	12,000-24,000
—	Caille Eclipse Floor Wheel 1904	$6000-11,000
30	Caille Big Six Lone Star Twin Floor Wheel 1904	$24,000-32,000
—	Caille Big Six Floor Wheel 1904	$7000-12,000
31	Caille Big Six Special Floor Wheel 1904	$11,000-15,000
32	Caille RouletteFloor Machine 1904	$24,000-30,000
—	Caille Venus Floor Wheel 1907	$14,000-25,000
—	Caille Centaur Triplet Floor Wheel 1907	$25,000-40,000
—	Caille Peerless Roulette Floor Machine 1907	$20,000-40,000
33	Caille Centaur Floor Wheel 1907	$7000-11,000
—	Caille Victor Floor Wheel 1907	$11,000-20,000
—	Caille Ben Hur Counter Wheel 1908	$2,000-3,800
—	Caille Lion Floor Wheel 1908	$7000-13,000
—	Caille Tourist Counter Machine 1912	$6000-12,000
—	Caille Silver Cup Counter Wheel 1912	$7000-13,000
—	Caille Operator Bell (Wood) 1916	$7000-13,000
27	Caille Victory Mint Vendor Bell 1920	$2500-5000
—	Caille Victory Bell 1920	$2500-5000
—	Caille Superior Bell (Naked Lady) 1926	$1400-2700
—	Caille Superior Mint Vendor Bell 1926	$1800-3500
34	Caille Superior Jackpot Bell 1928	$1100-2200
—	Caille Aristocrat Roulette Counter Machine 1932	$3500-7000
35	Caille Silent Sphinx Bell 1932	$1300-2500
—	Caille Dictator Bell 1934	$600
—	Caille Dough Boy Bell 1935	$600-1200
36	Caille Cadet Bell 1936	$600-1200

**Bally Spark Plug
Counter Machine
1934**

Bally Spark Plug makes up in uniqueness what it lost in beauty.
It's a payout simulated horserace with great action.

POOR	FAIR	GOOD	EXCELLENT
$1500	$2000	$2500	$3000

**Buckley Extra Award
Crisscross Bell
1948**

Buckley was one of the companies that made a fair-sized inroad with
revamp machines. They used Mills' mechanisms and added their
own unique front.

POOR	FAIR	GOOD	EXCELLENT
$700	$900	$1100	$1400

Buckley Bones
1936

Bones is an amazing machine; it's a countertop payout-type slot machine on which the player actually plays a game of craps. Two sets of spinning disks on the top roll actual dice. Four successive 7's or 11's would win the player a 100 point gold award. Bones, and Bally's Reliance were actually made by the same company, and they are very similar. Bones, however, are considered to be more rare, and are therefore more desirable.

POOR	FAIR	GOOD	EXCELLENT
$2500	$3300	$4100	$5000

C & F Baby Grand
1931

Miniature machines were popular in the 1930's because they could easily be hidden away when the heat was on. The only machine available that was smaller, was the Mills Vest Pocket, that was on the market at a later date. Amazingly enough, even with the diminutive size, this machine still had a jackpot.

POOR	FAIR	GOOD	EXCELLENT
$1000	$1300	$1600	$1900

Caille Victory Mint
Vendor Bell
1920

Collectors have been known to swoon over this machine. The feature that makes this ornate Caille so unique is its center-pull handle. Victory was also available in a no vendor model with lovely ladies on both sides of the operating arm.

POOR	FAIR	GOOD	EXCELLENT
$2,500	$3,300	$4,100	$5,000

Caille Detroit
Floor Wheel
1898

Caille Detroit is one of the first of the upright one reelers. Detroit featured a 6-way play action which allowed the bettor a number of betting options. Essentially the name of the game was to pick the color the wheel would land on. The player could hedge his bet by picking more than one color.

POOR	FAIR	GOOD	EXCELLENT
$6000	$6800	$7600	$9500

Caille New Century Detroit
Floor Wheel
1901

Caille was a big leader in upright machines, and the New Century Detroit is a model that is greatly sought after by collectors. The name New Century came from the fact that the country was heading into the 20th century. New Century was decorated with beautifully ornate castings and quarter sawn oak.

POOR	FAIR	GOOD	EXCELLENT
$8500	$9800	$11,100	$12,500

29

Caille Big Six Lone Star Twin
Floor Wheel
1904

Caille incorporated two of their best machines into one with the Big Six and the Lone Star combination. This model also sported a music box. If the local lawman was concerned about gambling, the operation could just point to the music box, and say the machine gave entertainment for the money inserted in its slots. This beautiful machine featured copper plated castings and a beautiful quarter sawn oak cabinet.

POOR	FAIR	GOOD	EXCELLENT
$24,000	$26,600	$29,200	$32,000

Caille Big Six Special Floor Wheel
1904

Caille machines have always been popular with collectors because of their beautiful castings and rich cabinets. One quick look at the Big Six Special will bear this out. This rare Special was a variation of the Big Six with larger color spaces. It's interesting to note that almost all of the manufacturers copied each other; Mills and Watling also produced Big Six, with Watling being the originator of the Big Six theme.

POOR	FAIR	GOOD	EXCELLENT
$11,000	$12,300	$13,600	$15,000

Caille Roulette Floor Machine
1904

Caille Roulette is a highly coveted machine by collectors. The game was unique in that it was a roulette concept as opposed to the upright wheel of fortune theme that was much more common. There were a number of betting combinations similar to the other upright games, except the payout was based on where the roulette ball landed.

POOR	FAIR	GOOD	EXCELLENT
$24,000	$26,000	$28,000	$30,000

Caille Centaur Floor Wheel
1907

The Caille Centaur is a beautiful machine with its rich ornate castings that are a Caille trademark. It sported a jackpot which was to resurface later in 3 reeler machines with great popularity. Notice the beautiful, cast claw feet.

POOR	FAIR	GOOD	EXCELLENT
$7,000	$8,300	$9,600	$11,000

Caille Superior Jackpot - Bell
1928

Caille machines are noted for their classic lines. The Superior can best be described as rich looking; the type of gambling device one would expect to find in a gentleman's club. The Superior Jackpot model is a takeoff from the Superior which featured a revealing female figure on the front. Caille mechanisms were somewhat less reliable than their dependable Mills counterparts.

POOR	FAIR	GOOD	EXCELLENT
$1,100	$1,400	$1,800	$2,200

Caille Silent Sphinx Bell
1932

Caille has always been noted for their classy looking machines. While the Sphinx is not as ornate as earlier machines, it has a certain rich feeling. Painted in its bright colors, it's hard to pass by without inserting a nickel.

POOR	FAIR	GOOD	EXCELLENT
$1,300	$1,700	$2,100	$2,500

Caille Cadet - Bell
1936

Dynamic styling is evident in the streamlined Cadet, with its unique circular jackpot. The Cadet also featured an escalator that moved from the bottom up and dropped the top coin into the coin tube. This machine was the last of a long line of beautiful and unique gambling devices. Caille Bros. of Detroit went out of business, soon after the Cadet was introduced.

POOR	FAIR	GOOD	EXCELLENT
$600	$800	$1,000	$1,200

Evans/Mills Conversion Bell
circa 1927

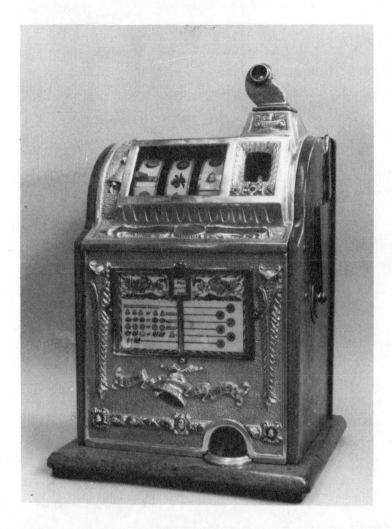

Look closely at this machine and the Mills trademarks are evident. This popular cabinet was offered by Fey, Mills, Rockola, and Evans. Evans was a large mail order house in Chicago. This machine is a representative of the popular Liberty Bell style.

POOR	FAIR	GOOD	EXCELLENT
$1,300	$1,700	$2,600	$3,100

F.W. Mills Mint Vendor
Counter Machine
1911

This gorgeous single reeler greatly resembles the Eagle Square Deal. Notice the outstanding graphics on the pay card.

POOR	FAIR	GOOD	EXCELLENT
$5,000	$6,600	$8,200	$10,000

Field Four Jacks
1929

The Jacks machines have been very popular over the years. People just love to watch the pennies they launch through the play field. Theoretically there is some skill involved in landing a coin in the jackpot slot. The name Jacks is just an abbreviation for jackpot.

POOR	FAIR	GOOD	EXCELLENT
$500	$660	$820	$1,000

Fey Liberty Bell
1905

The Fey Liberty Bell is a legend, because it was the first 3 reel payout-type slot machine. It was invented by Charles Fey, of San Francisco. Note the symbols are not the familiar bell/fruit type that were later introduced by Mills. Finding one of these is like finding a 3 pound gold nugget.

POOR	FAIR	GOOD	EXCELLENT
$28,000	$31,500	$35,000	$38,000

Fey 3 Jacks
circa 1910

This type machine was produced by several different makers: Clauson, Fey, Field, and finally, Rockola. Rockola probably had the largest share of the market with their 3 Jacks, 4 Jacks, and 5 Jacks models. The Clauson and Fey machines are the rarest of the group. Players flipped their coin into a field of pins. The coin danced through the pins to the bottom, and if it ended up in the jackpot slot, there was a winner.

POOR	FAIR	GOOD	EXCELLENT
$600	$800	$1,000	$1,200

Groetchen-Columbia Bell
1936

The Columbia Bell is a unique little machine. One feature that is particularly interesting is an interchangeable coin setup. It could be easily set up to take pennies, nickels, dimes or quarters. Because of its small size it was great for counters. Of course, the small size was also great for hiding it away. Groetchen made a great many varieties of this machine in a long production run.

POOR	FAIR	GOOD	EXCELLENT
$550	$730	$910	$1,100

Jennings Operator Bell
1920

Amongst all of the cast iron and aluminum fronts, Jennings came out with a wood front machine. There's a good possibility that this was done to save money. However, the effect is one of richness and overall beauty. Jennings was a popular manufacturer and a lot of it had to do with their solid, dependable mechanisms.

POOR	FAIR	GOOD	EXCELLENT
$1,300	$1,700	$2,100	$2,500

Jennings Today Vendor Bell
1926

Why four columns of mints? More than likely Jennings wanted to make the machine look more like a vending machine than a gambling device. The manufacturer's greatest challenge was to keep their machines under the veil of legality. Without that, their market was severely cut. Note the familiar Jennings Dutch boy cast on the front of the machine.

POOR	FAIR	GOOD	EXCELLENT
$1,000	$1,300	$1,600	$2,000

Jennings Jackpot Bell
1929

Jennings Jackpot Bell is more commonly referred to as the Dutch Boy. Note the model shown was originally set up with a side vendor. The front paycard very specifically says the machine is a vendor and not a gambling device. Bright blue made the two Dutch boys stand out, creating an eye catching machine.

POOR	FAIR	GOOD	EXCELLENT
$1,000	$1,300	$1,600	$2,000

Jennings Electro
Vendor Bell
1930

Jennings introduced the world's first electric slot machine. It seemed like a great step in the progressive modernization of slot machines, but it was not readily accepted by the public. No one knows for sure why; possibly the players just didn't trust it. It came in both table model and floor models, both of which are practically extinct today.

POOR	FAIR	GOOD	EXCELLENT
$1,200	$1,600	$2,000	$2,400

Jennings New Victoria - Bell
1931

Jennings Victoria was designed with a conservative touch. Victoria's cabinet styling was also used on the Electrojax, one of the first electrically powered slots. While the Victoria isn't considered to be a classic, it is an attractive, reliable machine.

POOR	FAIR	GOOD	EXCELLENT
$900	$1,160	$1,420	$1,700

**Jennings New Victoria
Vendor Bell
1931**

Jennings gave this machine an art deco flavor, which seemed to show up in the jukeboxes of the period more than it did in slot machines. New Victoria was also available in a non-vendor front in all coin denominations.

POOR	FAIR	GOOD	EXCELLENT
$900	$1,160	$1,420	$1,700

**Jennings Victoria Silent Bell
1932**

Surprise! Surprise! This Victoria Silent was nicknamed the Peacock by operators. Restored with vivid colors, this machine is a knockout. Understandably, this model is very popular with collectors.

POOR	FAIR	GOOD	EXCELLENT
$1,500	$1,660	$1,820	$2,000

Jennings Sportsman Golf Ball Vendor Bell
1932

In the 1930's golf was the popular game of the in crowd. So bless Jennings' little inventive soul, they decided to produce a machine that would appeal to the golf set. This machine was the rage at the country club because it paid off in golf balls instead of money.

POOR	FAIR	GOOD	EXCELLENT
$1,100	$1,460	$1,820	$2,200

Jennings' Little Duke Bell
1932

Jennings' Little Duke was an all-time favorite early in the game with operators, and later, with collectors. It was marketed as a more affordable machine for the operator. Coin denominations were 1¢, 5¢, and 10¢ predominantly, which appealed to more conservative players. The unique features of the game were its small size, and the 3 spinning wheels instead of reels.

POOR	FAIR	GOOD	EXCELLENT
$1,300	$1,700	$2,100	$2,600

Jennings Silver Moon Chief
Bell 1941

Jennings seemed to be in a groove for a number of years in terms of the style and function of their machines. Although the Chief name is present on the Silver Moon, there is no sign of Indians on this machine. It's a great looking machine graphically.

POOR	FAIR	GOOD	EXCELLENT
$800	$1,060	$1,320	$1,600

Jennings Four Star Chief-Bell
1936

The Jennings Chief has beautiful graphics of two Indians on a hunt with pine trees in the background. The Chief series was the beginning of a long and successful run for Jennings. The Four Star and its predecessor, the One Star, are very similar in design. Both were available in vendor models.

POOR	FAIR	GOOD	EXCELLENT
$900	$1,200	$1,500	$1,800

Jennings Silver Chief-Bell
1937

The Silver Chief is part of Jennings' long running Chief series. Jennings felt that once they had a winning cabinet theme, they should stick with it. This model came with a chromed front, instead of polished aluminum.

POOR	FAIR	GOOD	EXCELLENT
$750	$1,000	$1,250	$1,500

Jennings Cig-A-Rola Bell
1937

Jennings Cig-A-Rola is a combination cigarette machine/slot machine. The machine could be operated as a simple cigarette vendor or a gambler could put his money in and take a chance at winning from 1 to 10 packs of his favorite brand. The machine may not be beautiful, but it certainly is unique.

POOR	FAIR	GOOD	EXCELLENT
$600	$800	$1,000	$1,200

Jennings Dixie Belle-Bell
1937

The Dixie Bell was a special order machine that was made for Harold's Club. It was named for Dixie Smith, the wife of the well-known owner of Harold's Club. Quite often larger casinos, even now, have machines with special themes made for their business.

POOR	FAIR	GOOD	EXCELLENT
$900	$1,200	$1,500	$1,800

Jennings Sportsman Golf Ball Vendor
1937

The machine pictured on right is the 1937 update of the earlier Sportsman on the left. The internal mechanism remained much the same. Jennings just streamlined the cabinet and placed the pay card at a jaunty angle.

POOR	FAIR	GOOD	EXCELLENT
$1,100	$1,400	$1,700	$2,100

Jennings Bronze Chief Bell
1941

Jennings was obviously into Indians. This is one of the many "chief" themes produced through the years. One of the highlights of this machine is the bronzed plate at the top, and the 2 large embossed stars.

POOR	FAIR	GOOD	EXCELLENT
$750	$1,000	$1,250	$1,500

Jennings
Lucky Chief Bell
1945

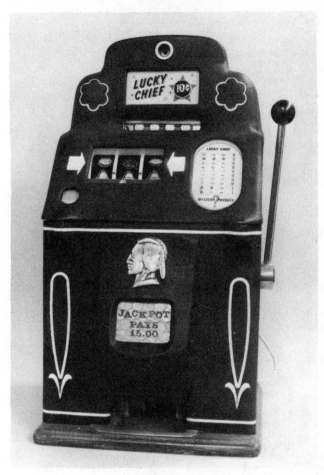

Lucky Chief is another of the series of Chiefs produced by Jennings for many years. The familiar polished casting of the Indian is on the front. The machine had a mystery payout that paid out when the player least expected it, theoretically. The question: Was the Chief lucky for the house, or for the player?

POOR	FAIR	GOOD	EXCELLENT
$650	$850	1,050	$1,300

Jennings Standard Chief Bell
1946

Jennings Standard Chief is a classic in a sense. While it is not beautiful, it is a machine that many old timers recognize as a standard, much like the Mills Hightop. The mechanism is considered to be one of the most reliable ever built.

POOR	FAIR	GOOD	EXCELLENT
$700	$900	$1,100	$1,400

Jennings Export Chief - Bell
1949

The Export Chief is essentially the same as the Standard Chief. The Export model was set up for foreign coinage, and the Standard Chief was set up for American coinage. Collectors, of course, will pay more for the Standard Chief. Both machines are noted for their reliable mechanisms.

POOR	FAIR	GOOD	EXCELLENT
$500	$660	$820	$1,000

Jennings Governor Bell
1964

Jennings carried their Indian theme right down to the 1960's. This Governor model has a tic tac toe theme that was first used by Jennings in 1948. Tic tac toe meant that players could win on diagonal as well as horizontal combinations of the tic tac toe symbols. This is an exciting game to play because of all of the possible winning combinations.

POOR	FAIR	GOOD	EXCELLENT
$550	$730	$910	$1,100

**Maley Investor
circa 1895**

This drop coin machine shows the grand design that is found in many early machines. The Investor is so classy looking that it almost does look like an investment to drop your money inside.

POOR	FAIR	GOOD	EXCELLENT
$1,200	$1,600	$2,000	$2,500

**Mills Jackpot - Bell
(Poinsettia)
1929**

Jackpot got its name obviously because of the jackpot. Sell was the name of the game with slot machines, and a great inducement to the customer was a visible pot full of coins that could be won. This machine, nicknamed the Poinsettia, was the second model of the Jackpot series.

POOR	FAIR	GOOD	EXCELLENT
$1,200	$1,600	$2,000	$2,500

Mills Dewey Floor Wheel
1899

The Dewey was a successful machine for Mills and was produced for many years. It sported a likeness of Admiral Dewey who was a patriot of the time. Cabinet styles were changed several times over the years.

POOR	FAIR	GOOD	EXCELLENT
$5,000	$6,1000	$7,200	$8,500

Mills 20th Century Floor Wheel
1900

The end of the 1800's brought on a new age that was our 20th century. Mills knew that the country had high hopes for the 20th century, so they decided it would be a great theme for one of their machines. American marketing has always been a new improved model, and that's what the 20th Century Floor Wheel was about.

POOR	FAIR	GOOD	EXCELLENT
$8,000	$9,300	$10,600	$12,000

Mills Cricket Floor Machine
1904

Mills Cricket is a relatively simple machine based on a principle that resurfaced many times in other gambling machines. The bettor's coin was flipped into a play field of pins and jumped either in to jackpot or a loser's slot. It looked very easy, and was therefore very tempting; however, usually the coin found its way into the lost slot. This is an infectious game that people love to play.

POOR	FAIR	GOOD	EXCELLENT
$8,000	$10,300	$12,600	$15,000

Mills Big Six Floor Wheel
1904

Don't be surprised to also see a Watling Big Six, and a Caille Big Six. The original was Watling, but it was quickly copied by other manufacturers. The Six theme comes from 6 numbered, and color coded payoff combinations.

POOR	FAIR	GOOD	EXCELLENT
$8,000	$9,300	$10,600	$12,000

Mills Operator Bell
1910

This cast iron, metal sided Operator Bell is a direct descendant of the Liberty Bell. Operators were businessmen who purchased machines, convinced other businessmen to allow them to place a machine at their place of business, and then shared in the profits. Mills obviously knew which side their bread was buttered on by making this early machine for the operators.

POOR	FAIR	GOOD	EXCELLENT
$4,000	$5,200	$6,400	$7,500

Mills O.K. Vendor - Bell
1922

Generally this machine will be found with a candy vendor on the side. If the vendor isn't there, look for several telltale holes. The O.K. name meant the machine was O.K. for use in non-gambling sports, such as general stores, barber shops, drug stores, etc. The O.K. did this by having the vending feature and a no value type token payout. The little window above the paycard let the player know in advance if the next play was a win or a lose.

POOR	FAIR	GOOD	EXCELLENT
$1,300	1,700	$2,100	$2,600

Mills Front O.K. - Bell
1923

Slot machine manufacturers were always thinking up ways to get around the gambling laws. The O.K. featured a window that told if the player would win on the next play. Since the player knew he was going to win or lose, the machine was considered to be legal. Notice the 4 columns of mints which allowed the machine to be touted as a vending machine.

POOR	FAIR	GOOD	EXCELLENT
$1,100	$1,700	$2,100	$2,600

Mills Jackpot - Bell
(Torchfront)
1928

Quickly nicknamed The Torchfront because of its torches on either side of the jackpot, this machine was the first of the Mills Jackpot series. Jackpots were features that were included for many years on most machines, because of their great appeal to the clientele.

POOR	FAIR	GOOD	EXCELLENT
$1,200	$1,600	$2,000	$2,500

Mills Baseball Vendor Bell
1929

Baseball is a truly unique concept in skirting the law and entertaining the customer. The front of this vendor allows for manual scoring of a baseball game. With each spin of the reels, instructions were given for a baseball play. The law was satisfied in that it was a baseball game, not a gambling machine, and the customer was given an additional entertainment feature.

POOR	FAIR	GOOD	EXCELLENT
$1,600	$2,100	$2,600	$3,200

Mills Silent Bell (War Eagle)
1931

These popular machines are more commonly known as the War Eagle. This was the first of the escalator models with five coins visibly moving along at the top. Mills used the name Silent because it was an improved machine with much quieter operation.

POOR	FAIR	GOOD	EXCELLENT
$1,400	$1,860	$2,320	$2,800

Mills-Silent F.O.K.
1931

F.O.K., or Front O.K., meant that the machine had a vendor which made the machine legal, or O.K. In an effort to get around gambling laws, this model was suggested to be a vendor only. The idea was that it vended mints and paid off in trade tokens. Theoretically the vendor portion could not be disconnected or altered.

POOR	FAIR	GOOD	EXCELLENT
$1,200	$1,600	$2,000	$2,400

Mills Silent Gooseneck - Bell
(Wolfs head)
1931

This popular machine has several nicknames, however The Lion's Head or Front is the most common. The Silent Gooseneck was produced along with The Silent. The mechanisms were essentially the same, but the Silent Gooseneck retained the Gooseneck that was prevalent in earlier Mills machines.

POOR	FAIR	GOOD	EXCELLENT
$1,500	$2,000	$2,500	$3,000

Mills Silent Golden - Bell
(Roman Head)
1932

The Mills Silent Golden is more popularly known as the Roman's Head. The Silent Golden name came from the silent mechanism and the gold award feature. Mills marketing genius was next to none and the gold award idea was readily accepted by the public. The idea was to hit 3 gold award symbols, thereby winning the gold award token which exceeded the jackpot in value. The unique graphics on this machine has made it very popular with collectors.

POOR	FAIR	GOOD	EXCELLENT
$1,400	$1,900	$2,400	$2,800

Mills Mystery - Bell
(Castle Front)
1933

This machine was popularly known as the Blue Front due to its dramatic dark blue background. The name mystery came from the 3 - 5 payout instead of the earlier 2 - 4 payout. Winners were mystified when they won 3 coins instead of 2, or 5 instead of 4. Large numbers of this machine were produced, so don't be surprised if one turns up in an unlikely spot.

POOR	FAIR	GOOD	EXCELLENT
$900	$1,200	$1,500	$1,800

Mills Extraordinary - Bell
1933

What's so extraordinary about it? It reflected the hope of the new age of modern inventions. The distinctive art deco case was meant to represent technological achievement. It also went under the alias of Gray Front due to its military gray background. Extraordinary was a popular machine that resurfaced as an upright cabinet model in 1938, called the Extraordinary Club Bell.

POOR	FAIR	GOOD	EXCELLENT
$900	$1,200	$1,500	$1,800

Mills Silent Bell Gooseneck
(Skyscraper)
1933

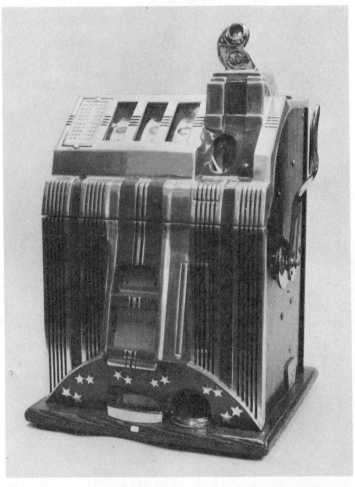

What was Mills doing with a gooseneck in 1933 when they started producing their horizontal coin excalator in 1931? Apparently someone found a huge quantity of goosenecks laying around doing nothing, and they decided to put their last gooseneck into production.

POOR	FAIR	GOOD	EXCELLENT
$900	$1,200	$1,500	$1,900

Mills Q.T. Bell
(Firebird)
1934

Firebird is the first of the Mills' Q.T. Models. Later they changed to the plain front which was produced in larger numbers. They were usually in 1¢ or 5¢ denominations, and could often be found on display counters, or near cash registers in the 1930's. The psychology of this was much like the gum racks and magazine racks of today. Customers were expected to, and often did part with their extra change at these points of purchase.

POOR	FAIR	GOOD	EXCELLENT
$900	$1,200	$1,500	$1,800

Mills Q.T. - Bell
1936

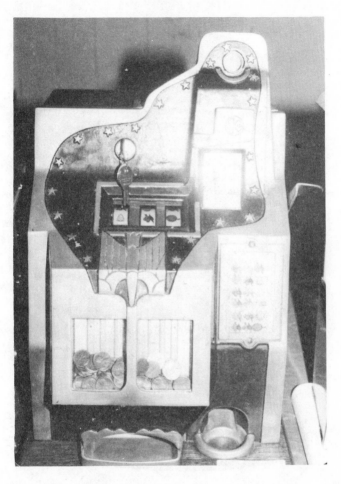

The Q.T. was Mills' major entry into the small-sized slot machine market, although they did produce another smaller machine called the Vest Pocket. Q.T. was an excellent size for slipping under the counter when the heat was on. Remember the expression "on the Q.T." (or on the sly)? It was also useful to operators with limited space requirements. The machine was sometimes coined as the Green Front due to its green color.

POOR	FAIR	GOOD	EXCELLENT
$850	$1,130	$1,410	$1,700

Mills Futurity Bell
1936

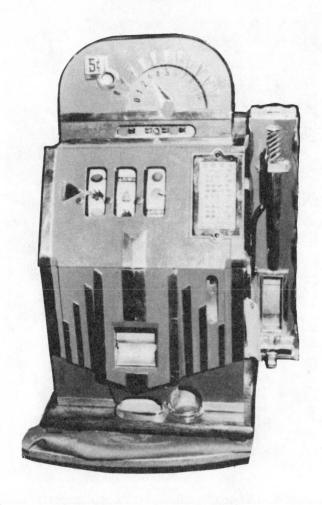

Futurity seemed to be a can't lose machine; the counter advanced on each play that didn't payout. If the player made 10 passes without any payouts, the machine would give him back all 10 coins. The only catch was getting all the way to 9, and hitting a small payout, because then the counter went back to 0.

POOR	FAIR	GOOD	EXCELLENT
$1,400	$1,860	$2,320	$2,800

Mills Cherry - Bell
(Bursting Cherry)
1937

The Cherry got its name from its extra payout of 10 instead of 5 when 2 cherries and a bell or lemon turned up. The Cherry Bell is often confused with the Brown Front which has a similar appearance. Its most common nickname is the Bursting Cherry. Like most of the Mills line, it was produced in a variety of models which included a mint vendor model, and the one shown with an extra jackpot window.

POOR	FAIR	GOOD	EXCELLENT
$950	$1,150	$1,450	$1,900

Mills Bonus - Bell
(Horsehead)
1937

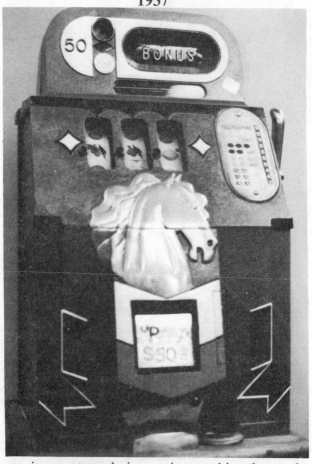

The Bonus is an extremely interesting machine due to the bonus feature. By turning up the letters B O N U S in sequence, the player received an 18 coin bonus. The benefit to the house is obvious in that it kept the player coming back for more. The only problem with the machine was its complicated mechanism which had a tendency to fail. The machine was nicknamed the Horsehead for obvious reasons. Note: The machine pictured was most likely an export due to 50¢ denomination; also, Bonus feature is missing.

POOR	FAIR	GOOD	EXCELLENT
$1,200	$1,600	$2,000	$2,400

Mills Brown Front - Bell
1938

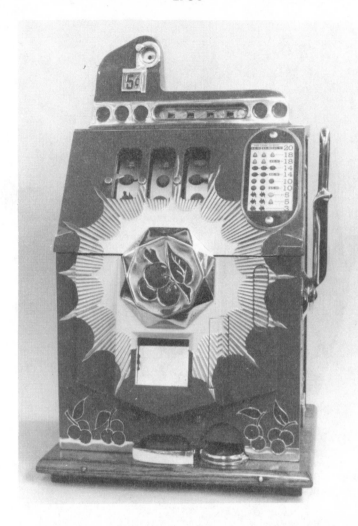

If the Brown Front looks exactly like the Cherry Bell, it's because they are the same cabinet. The main difference between them is that they are painted different colors. The background of the Brown Front is brown, highlighted by a burst of bright orange in the center.

POOR	FAIR	GOOD	EXCELLENT
$950	$1,150	$1,450	$1,900

Mills Vest Pocket
1938

Vest Pocket was Mills' smallest payout slot machine. It was purposely made boxey and plain to avoid attracting attention. Even the payout card flipped over to conceal the reels. Interestingly enough, the mechanism was a micro-version of the larger bell slots.

POOR	FAIR	GOOD	EXCELLENT
$250	$350	$450	$550

Mills Chrome Bell
(Diamond Front)
1939

Chrome Bell received its name because they came from the factory with a dazzling chrome front, although there were glitter-treated models, and other variations. The nickname that has caught on for this machine is the diamond front, because of the raised diamonds on both sides of the front. This was a successful machine saleswise, and it is considered to be very reliable mechanically.

POOR	FAIR	GOOD	EXCELLENT
$850	$1,150	$1,450	$1,700

Mills Q.T. Chrome Bell
(Sweetheart)
1941

It looks too innocuous to be a gambling device. The Q.T. was a very popular line for Mills and this is their 1941 update. Look at the heart shape at the top of the machine, which inspired the sweetheart nickname.

POOR	FAIR	GOOD	EXCELLENT
$900	$1200	$1500	$1800

Mills Golden Falls
1946

"Drenched with beauty! Flooded with mechanical improvements" was how the Golden Falls was described in some of the original advertising literature. They really had a way with words in those days.

POOR	FAIR	GOOD	EXCELLENT
$800	$1,060	$1,320	$1,600

Mills Black Cherry - Bell
1945

Black Cherry is noted for its dramatic raised cherries on the front casting. This machine is sought after by many beginning collectors because it has the look of a classic slot machine. Unfortunately, this machine is defined as illegal in states that have a 1941 cutoff date.

POOR	FAIR	GOOD	EXCELLENT
$800	$1,060	$1,320	$1,600

Mills Jewel - Bell
(777 Hightop)
1947

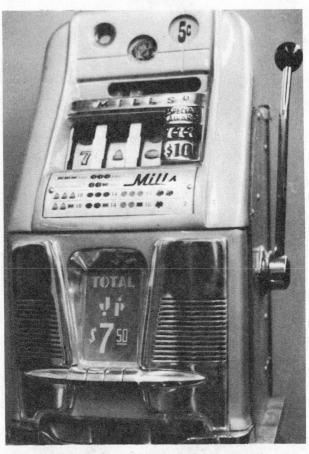

Mills Jewel - Bell is probably the most recognized slot machine ever produced. Because of its durability it is still in operation in many casinos throughout the world. The well-recognized nickname for this machine is the "hightop" due to its tall modular design. Beware of lookalikes; one very common one is the Sega made in Japan. The Hightop was made in a variety of models (the model pictured is the 777) and many of the clubs converted the cabinets to their own themes.

POOR	FAIR	GOOD	EXCELLENT
$750	$1,000	$1,250	$1,500

Mills Melon Bell
1948

A big, juicy colorful melon dominates the front of this Mills' Hightop. Mills made a number of variations of the Hightop. This happens to be one that doesn't turn up much.

POOR	FAIR	GOOD	EXCELLENT
$900	$1,200	$1,500	$1,800

Pace Bantam Bell
1928

Pace's Bantam Bell is the type of cute little machine that little old ladies would like to have setting on top of their Victrolas. It's so cheerful and gay looking, that no one would think badly of it for being involved in gambling. Bantam was sized down to appeal to the small machine market. There were plain fronts, jackpot fronts, and the jackpot vendor front pictured.

POOR	FAIR	GOOD	EXCELLENT
$900	$1,200	$1,500	$1,800

Mills - Golden Nugget
Revamp Bell   1955

The Golden Nugget Conversion is one of many conversions, or variations of the Mills Jewel Bell. The Golden Nugget Casino wanted their own distinctive slot machine so they converted the cabinet to their own theme. Be careful with conversions; some of the more popular ones have been reproduced. The one pictured above is a **reproduction!**

Original

POOR	FAIR	GOOD	EXCELLENT
$1,500	$2,000	2,500	$3,000

Reproduction

POOR	FAIR	GOOD	EXCELLENT
$900	$1,200	$1,500	$1,800

Pace Operator's Bell
1927

The Pace Operator's Bell was Pace's first entry into the slot machine business. Pace was a good salesman and his machines grabbed a strong foothold in the market. This machine's unique feature is the circular escalator that Pace continued to use in most of their machines.

POOR	FAIR	GOOD	EXCELLENT
$1,100	$1,460	$1,820	$2,100

Pace Star Revamp Bell
1933

Pace made conversion fronts for operators to change the look of older machines. This particular conversion was made for Mills' machines. The interior mechanism remained the same, so essentially these are Mills machines.

POOR	FAIR	GOOD	EXCELLENT
$950	$1,150	$1,450	$1,900

Pace Deluxe Chrome Comet - Bell
1939

The Pace Comet looks like it could get up and fly. Aerodynamic styling was a sign of things to come. Slot machines became more and more streamlined in design as time went on. The Comet was a successful, dependable machine and some are still in operation in various casinos.

POOR	FAIR	GOOD	EXCELLENT
$700	$900	$1,100	$1,400

Pace Star Bell
circa 1948

Pace machines can still be found in Harrah's Clubs today. Harrah's bought into the Pace organization and produced the 8 Star for use in their own clubs. This machine retains the circular coin escalator that is found on most Pace machines.

POOR	FAIR	GOOD	EXCELLENT
$650	$850	$1,050	$1,300

**Rex Electric Bell
1937**

When the Rex came out it was the smallest payout slot in production. That was quickly changed the next year when Mills introduced the Vest Pocket. It sold for $37.50 in lots of five.

POOR	FAIR	GOOD	EXCELLENT
$1,000	$1,300	$1,600	$2,000

**Superior Races
Counter Machine
1935**

This is the machine for someone who wants the truly unique. Three tiers of horses compete in a simulated horse race. The player is rewarded when 3 horses of the same color line up.

POOR	FAIR	GOOD	EXCELLENT
$1,800	$2,300	$2,800	$3,400

Rockola Reserve Jackpot Revamp Bell
1930

This machine is a Rockola - Jennings - Fey. The mechanism was produced by Jennings; the conversion front was produced by Rockola, and adapted to the Jennings mech. Charles Fey took the whole unit, ground off the Rockola name on the front, and added his own reel strips. This is an example of how machines and castings were used back and forth by the various companies.

POOR	FAIR	GOOD	EXCELLENT
$1,100	$1,500	$1,900	$2,200

Watling Brownie Counter Wheel
1900

The Brownie, which was produced by both Watling and Mills, is a countertop one reeler. It works much the same way as the coveted upright one reelers. Select a color category, drop in a coin, or coins, and if the correct color hit, there was a payout. The machine pictured is missing the all-important top coin acceptor piece.

POOR	FAIR	GOOD	EXCELLENT
$1,800	$2,400	$3,000	$3,600

Watling Jefferson Counter Wheel

Counter Wheels were the smaller counterparts to the upright floor wheels. The concept of the game was essentially the same; they were just made to go on a counter. Watling's Jefferson was a popular machine of the period, and is noted for its nice clean lines.

POOR	FAIR	GOOD	EXCELLENT
$2,500	$3,300	$4,100	$5,000

**Watling Blue Seal
Front Vender Bell
1927**

Watling's Blue Seal line seems to be the homely older sister when compared to the Treasury and Rol-a-tops which were later produced by the same manufacturer. All in all, the Blue Seals were very popular with operators because they worked well, and that was the name of the game.

POOR	FAIR	GOOD	EXCELLENT
$1,000	$1,300	$1,600	$2,000

**Watling - Blue Seal - Bell
(Jackpot Front Vendor)
1929**

The Blue Seal comes in a great variety of models: two column vendors, four column vendors, jackpot fronts, plain fronts, etc. It wasn't exactly a classic in terms of beauty, but it worked well, and held up even better. Of course, the Watling company was noted for their fine scales, so this was no great surprise.

POOR	FAIR	GOOD	EXCELLENT
$1,000	$1,300	$1,600	$2,000

Watling Twin Jackpot Bell
1931

The twin jackpot idea was used by a number of manufacturers. A winner would receive the first jackpot and normally the second jackpot was held in reserve for the next winner. This meant there was always a full jackpot and players could always be assured the possibility of winning a jackpot. This model was part of Watling's Blue Seal line.

POOR	FAIR	GOOD	EXCELLENT
$900	$1,200	$1,500	$1,800

**Watling Rol-a-Top Bell
(Coinfront Model)
1935**

Rol-a-Top, to say the least, is in great demand. The model shown is not particularly rare but collectors love them because of their outstanding graphics and the circular coin escalator. The first model of the long running machine was called the Rol-a-Tor. However, Watling eventually changed the name to Rol-a-Top. The machine has had several different front castings: The horn of plenty spilling out coins (illustrated above), a bird of paradise model with an outpouring of fruit, a mystery front model, similar to the Mills Mystery Bell, a Cherryfront, and a rare 5¢ - 25¢ model.

POOR	FAIR	GOOD	EXCELLENT
$2,000	$2,600	$3,300	$4,000

Watling Treasury Bell
1936

Watling's Treasury is even more sought after by collectors than the Rol-a-Top. Part of the reason, of course, is rarity: there are fewer Treasuries around than Rol-a-Tops. The other part is strong graphic appeal, with a bright yellow background featuring golden coins and an eagle over the jackpot.

POOR	FAIR	GOOD	EXCELLENT
$2,500	$3,300	$4,100	$5,000

Rol-A-Top Bell
(Bird of Paradise)
1938

All Rol-A-Tops are sought after by collectors. Of the many variations that were produced, it would be hard to pick a favorite, but the Bird of Paradise would be a contender. The castings of the Bird of Paradise feature an outpouring of fruit surrounding the Bird of Paradise. All painted in bright colors, it produces a beautiful effect.

POOR	FAIR	GOOD	EXCELLENT
$2,200	$3,000	$3,800	$4,500

VII: Trade Stimulators

Trade stimulators are mechanical games of chance that do not have an automatic money payout. They are based on an endless variety of themes that include spinning wheels of fortune, 5 reel poker games, dice games, roulette games, 21 games, 3 reel symbol games, one reel symbol games, penny drops, and the list goes on and on. They come in all shapes and sizes. The early machines were often ornate with beautiful cast iron and rich woods. Later machines made use of cast aluminum and liberal amounts of hardwood were also included on many models.

Trade stimulators began to appear on the scene in fairly large numbers in the 1890's. Basically, stimulators are fairly simple machines. Since they were not encumbered with payout mechanisms, the technology was available fairly early. The early machines were often tied into cigars. For example, the fairest wheel of the 1890's was typical of the type of stimulators found on cigar store counters. The customer inserted a nickel in the top, and set a wheel in motion. At the very least, he received a nickel cigar, and if the wheel landed on a 2 or 3, he would receive the equivalent amount of cigars. Who could pass up a deal like that? The store keeper was happy because this device helped to stimulate business, and the patron was happy, because he felt like he got something for nothing.

As time progressed, these machines became popular for bars, pool rooms, hardware stores, and other small businesses. Often trade stimulators were sitting on the counter next to the cash register. This marketing concept is very similar to the merchandise racks at checkout counters in today's stores. Since the customer is in a buying mood, the storekeeper hopes to get a little more of his pocket change.

During the Depression, trade stimulators shared the same popularity as slots. Businessmen had a hard way to go, and anything that helped to stimulate business was welcome. Machines were produced in great varieties during this period by a number of different manufacturers. Popularity began to slow in the 1940's, and by the 1950's, trade stimulators were all but extinct due to their illegality in many states, and lack of interest. One wonders even if they were legal today, if they would have a viable market.

For many years, trade stimulators were passed up by collectors in favor of payout-type slots. However, there is a growing interest in stimulators. Many auctions are showing increased prices and demand for these non-payout machines. Some of the early versions are commanding higher prices than popular 3 reeler payout machines.

The legality of collecting these machines is somewhat unclear. It is fairly well agreed upon that states allowing payout-type machines for collector purposes will allow trade stimulators. The best bet is to check the individual state laws before taking a chance. It's a shame that these unique momentos of our past are misunderstood by certain legislative and enforcement agencies.

This early photograph illustrates two old gents in a smoke shop. There is a Mills Commercial on the counter, and a Mills Jockey against the wall. The barber pole above indicates that a barber shop is in the back room.

In this early bar photograph, the trade stimulator is in the foreground, and is somewhat out of focus. It appears to be a Mills Royal Trader.

Organization has been changed in this section. In order to make locating a machine easier, they have been ordered as to type, such as five reeler machines, three reeler machines, dice machines, etc. This is as opposed to the chronological order used in the first edition.

TRADE STIMULATORS

ILLUS. PAGE NO.	MACHINE NAME	PRICE RANGE
119	Fey On The Level 1907	$1500-3500
120	Fey Midget 3 in 1 1926	$325-650
121	Ft. Wayne Novelty Little Joe Dicer 1934	$200-400
—	Gottlieb Indian Dice c. 1937	$350-700
—	Groetchen Dice-o-Matic 1934	$150-300
—	Kalamazoo Automatic Kazoo 1935	$125-250
—	Mills I Will 1904	$3000-6000
—	Mills Crap Shooter c. 1907	$1250-2500
—	Mills 36 Lucky Spot 1926	$250-500
122	Pioneer Novelty Big Bones 1933	$200-400
122	Quality Supply Horses c. 1945	$100-175
164	Witney Seven Grand c. 1939	$250-500

FIVE REELER MACHINES

—	Bally Baby 1936	$125-250
—	Buckley Pilgrim 1934	$200-400
—	Caille Quintette 1901	$4500-9000
—	Caille Royal Jumbo 1901	$750-1500
123	Caille Good Luck 1902	$500-1000
—	Caille Reliance 1904	$1250-2500
—	Caille Globe 1906	$3000-6000
—	Caille Banker 1906	$1250-2500
—	Canda Success 1895	$900-1800
—	Canda Jumbo c. 1897	$1200-2500
—	Canda Jumbo Giant 1897	$1800-3500
—	Canda Automatic Card Machine c. 1898	$1250-2500
—	Canda Jumbo Success c. 1899	$800-1600
124	Canda Perfection Card Machine 1900	$550-1100
—	Clune Commercial 1900	$1250-2500
123	Daval Chicago Club House 1932	$250-500
—	Daval Reel 21 1936	$150-300
125	Daval Joker Gum Vendor 1938	$175-350
—	Daval Ace 1940	$100-200

111

Kitzmiller's Automatic Salesman
circa 1920

The penny drop machines were produced in great numbers. In the first place, the games were simple; the customer didn't have to be a genius to learn how to play. They were also simple mechanically. There wasn't much that could go wrong, since there were so few moving parts. The player flipped his penny into the playing field, where it bounced through a series of pins. In this particular game, the penny passed through a color-coded target, and was awarded accordingly.

POOR	FAIR	GOOD	EXCELLENT
$250	$325	$400	$500

Little Dream Gum Machine
circa 1922

Little Dream is another of the very popular penny-drop machines. The player received a gumball for every penny. The game was pictured as a baseball game with outs and runs. Of course, the operator could easily convert the run multiples to payout factors. It's also interesting to note that the pennies usually landed in the out slots.

POOR	FAIR	GOOD	EXCELLENT
$200	$270	$340	$400

**Mills New Target Practice
1925**

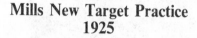

Mills Target Practice was Mills' contribution to the penny drop market. The machine was cast with two discus players on the front; very macho. As with all of the other penny drops, the penny bounced through a playing field and into a slot that was good for a payout, or a thank you, maybe next time.

POOR	FAIR	GOOD	EXCELLENT
$350	$450	$550	$650

**Standard Amusement
Windmill
circa 1943**

Standard Amusement features the very popular coin drop game. The scene is a little unusual, however, in that it depicts a Dutch scene with, of course, a windmill.

POOR	FAIR	GOOD	EXCELLENT
$175	$225	$300	$350

Robbins Baseball
circa 1933

The penny drop theme was used and revised by many manufacturers. Flip a penny into the playing field, and it would bounce through the pins and drop into a slot with or without a point value. This machine was set up with a baseball theme, but there was also an underlying point system that allowed for wagering.

POOR	FAIR	GOOD	EXCELLENT
$200	$260	$320	$400

Exhibit Supply
Get A Pack
1933

Exhibit Supply's Get A Pack was an easy game to play. Two dice were spun and if they showed either a 7 or an 11 the player received one or two packs of cigarettes. A gumball was also vended every time.

POOR	FAIR	GOOD	EXCELLENT
$125	$165	$205	$250

Fey On the Level

All machines produced by Charles Fey are in great demand, and the On The Level is one of the most sought after. It is made of heavy cast iron and either came painted, or with a nickel finish. The player pushed the plunger, setting the dice in a spin, and then won or lost according to the payout card.

POOR	FAIR	GOOD	EXCELLENT
$1,500	$2,200	$2,900	$3,500

Fey Midget
1926

There seems to be a great number of variations on the Fey Midget. Unfortunately very few of them have Fey cast on the mechanism. Marshal Fey, the great grandson of Charles Fey speculates that this is because most of the machines were made for independent operators. Also, Charles may have been trying to avoid possible legal problems for providing gambling machines. As an aside, Marshall Fey operates the Liberty Bell Saloon and Restaurant in Reno, Nevada, and has some of his grandfather's machines on view. It's a great place to visit.

POOR	FAIR	GOOD	EXCELLENT
$325	$425	$525	$650

Gottlieb Indian Dice
circa 1937

Unfortunately this is a rare little jewel. Very few of these machines turn up, and it is a shame because it's really a fun game. This is very similar to playing poker dice which is popular today in many taverns where people shake the dice for drinks.

POOR	FAIR	GOOD	EXCELLENT
$350	$450	$550	$700

Ft. Wayne Novelty
Little Joe Dicer
1934

Little Joe Dicer was a product of the Ft. Wayne Novelty Company. The concept was much the same as the Fey Midget, and other 6 dice spinners. For a 1¢, 5¢, or 10¢ bet the player pulled the handle, setting the spinner into motion. The total number showing on the 6 dice was added and compared to the pay card. The hardest combinations, such as 6 of a kind, paid the most.

POOR	FAIR	GOOD	EXCELLENT
$200	$275	$350	$400

**Pioneer Novelty
Big Bones
1933**

Big Bones is a unique concept, in that it's a coin-operated chuck-a-luck. A coin trips a release that lets the player turn the glass chuck-a-luck cage. Payoffs are designated on the front paycard. The left upper corner on this example displays a handwritten license number that more than likely was phony.

POOR	FAIR	GOOD	EXCELLENT
$200	$275	$350	$400

**Quality Supply Horses
circa 1945**

Don't be confused by the fact that this paycard says Hi-Low Seven. "Horses" had eight different paycards the operators could change at will to make a new game. This helped to keep the patrons from getting bored.

POOR	FAIR	GOOD	EXCELLENT
$100	$125	$150	$175

**Caille Good Luck
1902**

Fortunately a good part of the beautiful Good Luck decal is still visible on this machine. The ornate upper casting sets this machine apart as a Caille.

POOR	FAIR	GOOD	EXCELLENT
$500	$650	$800	$1,000

**Daval
Chicago Club House
1932**

Chicago Club House is a reel-type poker game. The 5 reels spun out a game of 5 card poker. Winning hands were shown on the payout card.

POOR	FAIR	GOOD	EXCELLENT
$250	$325	$400	$500

Canda Perfection Card Machine
1900

If this machine looks similar to the Mills Perfection, it's because they are essentially the same machine. Mills Novelty took over the Canda Company and made this popular machine part of their line. The player was given a poker hand with a spin of the 5 reels, and was paid according to how good the hand was.

POOR	FAIR	GOOD	EXCELLENT
$550	$730	$910	$1,100

**Daval Joker Gum Vendor
1938**

Daval Joker added a feature that was missing in most other five-reeler poker games. That, of course, was the joker, or wild card. This helped to push the odds in the player's favor, and made the game a lot more fun.

POOR	FAIR	GOOD	EXCELLENT
$175	$235	$295	$350

**Daval Ace
1940**

Small counter games such as the Ace were seen in large numbers in the 1940's. The concept of this game was a poker hand dealt out by the spinning reels: A straight flush paid the highest. Daval produced a similar machine that had 3 cigarette reels.

POOR	FAIR	GOOD	EXCELLENT
$100	$130	$160	$200

**Daval 21
circa 1941**

For such a little package, Daval's 21 packed a lot of play. For 1¢ the player spun the reels, and was shown 2 cards. Pushing buttons 3 and 4 would reveal 2 more cards. After this sequence, the House button was pushed, and the winner decided.

POOR	FAIR	GOOD	EXCELLENT
$125	$165	$205	$250

**Garden City Novelty
Army 21 Game
1936**

Army 21 is a great game to play because the player has more to do than just spin the reels. On the first spin, the player's first 2 cards were shown. Then they had the option of taking one, or two more cards, by pressing the option buttons. Finally, the dealer's hand button was pressed to reveal the winner. This machine was a product of the Garden City Novelty Company.

POOR	FAIR	GOOD	EXCELLENT
$275	$375	$475	$550

**Groetchen
Pok-O-Reel Triplex
1934**

Pok-O-Reel is a 5 reel poker hand theme. According to the paycard, various hands are good for free plays. Of course, everyone knew this was for an over the counter payout. Groetchen changed the size and shape of the machine several times over the years, and finished with a fairly small machine.

POOR	FAIR	GOOD	EXCELLENT
$225	$350	$375	$450

**Groetchen 21 Vendor
1934**

Groetchen 21 is a diversion from the usual 3 reel type machines. It is a five reel 21 game. When the reels are spun, 3 of the reels get covered up leaving 2 in view. The player can then hit with up to 3 cards, or stay.

POOR	FAIR	GOOD	EXCELLENT
$275	$375	$475	$550

Groetchen High Tension
circa 1934

High tension is very similar in cabinet style to its cousin the 21 Vendor. The game theme is horseracing. Three reels spun, one letter each to spell out a horse's name. If a winning horse turned up, the odds and place finished were shown on the other 2 reels. For the winner it was a payout across the counter and the loser received a gumball.

POOR	FAIR	GOOD	EXCELLENT
$300	$400	$500	$600

The Kelley
1903

The Kelley is a super-looking little machine. The front is quarter-sawn oak with a beautiful casting announcing the machine as a Kelley, Chicago Illinois. The object of the game was simple; add up the numbers showing on the reels, and if they equal one of the winning numbers on the paycard, there's a winner. The model shown is the stick gum vendor type.

POOR	FAIR	GOOD	EXCELLENT
$1,000	$1,300	$1,600	$2,000

Jennings Card Machine
circa 1935

This wood cabinet machine appears to be older than it really is. The lack of aluminum castings is fairly unusual in post-1920's machines. Poker was, of course, the theme of the game.

POOR	FAIR	GOOD	EXCELLENT
$450	$600	$750	$900

Mills Success
1901

Success was a very apropos name since this machine was produced for a number of years by several different manufacturers. The player inserted a nickel and spun the reels for a random poker hand.

POOR	FAIR	GOOD	EXCELLENT
$600	$800	$1000	$1200

Mills Upright Perfection
1901

The Perfection marquee advertised free cigars. For 5¢ the player spun the reels to show a poker hand. The better the hand, the more cigars the patron won. This game could also be played between several customers. Notice the beautiful quarter-sawn owk, and the face cast on the front.

POOR	FAIR	GOOD	EXCELLENT
$700	$900	$1100	$1300

Mills Little Perfection No. 2
1926

This Little Perfection is a variation of the 1901 Perfection. The latter model was changed into a flat sided cabinet, similar to many other stimulators of the day. Both games were 5 reelers, that spun out varieties of poker hands. Obviously the better the hand, the better the payout.

POOR	FAIR	GOOD	EXCELLENT
$400	$550	$650	$800

Mills Kounter King
1938

In 1938 the Kounter King sold for $25.00. Just about everyone would like to have one at that price today. The player tried to match a selection number by pushing a button to open a shutter. The more he matched, the higher the odds. It's like playing "Let's Make A Deal".

POOR	FAIR	GOOD	EXCELLENT
$200	$275	$350	$400

**National Draw Poker
1934**

This art deco-styled poker machine doesn't show up very often. National was one of the lesser-known manufacturers, and they weren't produced in high numbers.

POOR	FAIR	GOOD	EXCELLENT
$350	$450	$600	$750

**Pace New Deal
1935**

It gets a little confusing, but both Pace and Pierce made the New Deal. Essentially they are the same machine. The example shown features a jackpot which paid out on 3 deuces. This was not an automatic payout, however; it was controlled by the machine tender. The game theme is 5 card poker, and the paycard on the front of the machines shows the payoffs.

	Pace		
POOR	FAIR	GOOD	EXCELLENT
$250	$325	$400	$500
	Pierce		
$200	$275	$350	$400

Rockola Hold and Draw
1934

Rockolo's Hold and Draw advertises 2 spins for one coin. This interesting machine, with its distinctive art deco case is great fun to play. On every spin, the skill buttons can be pressed to stop each reel, thus revealing a poker hand. The player has 2 shots at getting a good hand. Of course, what makes the game fun, is the involvement of pushing the skill buttons.

POOR	FAIR	GOOD	EXCELLENT
$250	$330	$410	$500

Sittman and Pitt Card Machine
circa 1900

This little beauty had five revolving cylinders with an actual miniature deck of cards attached. The cylinder spun in a random fashion (after the player inserted a coin and pushed the plunger) and a poker hand was shown. With a pair on up, the winner received cigars according to the pay card. The machine was manufactured by Sittman Pitt of New York. However, don't be surprised to see some other jobber or dealer listed on nameplate, paycard, etc.

POOR	FAIR	GOOD	EXCELLENT
$1,300	$1,800	$2,300	$2,750

Buckley Horses
1935

Buckley Horses makes use of 4 reels to stimulate gambling at the track. After the player placed his bet, he pulled the handle and gave the reels a spin. If one of the horses on the paycard spelled out on the reels, the winner received the odds amount times the bet.

POOR	FAIR	GOOD	EXCELLENT
$250	$325	$400	$500

**Garden City Novelty
Bar Boy
1936**

There's no hiding the fact that this machine was made for tavern locations. The first reel on the machine was the odds reel, and the other 3 reels showed beer symbols. Matching 3 of a kind got the player the equivalent number of beers showing on the odds reel.

POOR	FAIR	GOOD	EXCELLENT
$200	$250	$300	$350

**Great States Mfg.
Sandy's Horses
1936**

Place your bet on a horse, release the handle, and the horse that finishes in front of the judge's stand is the winner. The paycard says you pay to see it operate, which is a little different than the usual non-gambling disclaimer. Sandy Horses was a product of Great States Manufacturing.

POOR	FAIR	GOOD	EXCELLENT
$275	$375	$475	$550

Mills Umpire
1905

Mills Umpire was based on the ever-popular baseball theme of the day. The player selected a color-coded play for a single, double, etc. If the reel stopped on a strike, out, or foul, it was a loss all the way around. The player had the option of hedging his bet on more than one option, which made the game quite interesting.

POOR	FAIR	GOOD	EXCELLENT
$2,500	$3,300	$4,100	$5,000

Mills Elk
1905

Betting from one to five coins varied the odds on this machine at the player's discretion. Winners were usually paid in drinks or cigars. The example shown is missing the marquee and the paycard and symbols are not original.

POOR	FAIR	GOOD	EXCELLENT
$2,000	$2,800	$3,600	$4,500

Mills Pilot
1906

Mills Pilot is a one reel game that was very similar in concept to the upright floor wheels. The player could bet from one to six coins, and if one of the symbols chosen showed up on the single reel, there was a payoff, usually in trade checks. Notice the beautiful nautical scenes on the castings.

POOR	FAIR	GOOD	EXCELLENT
$2,500	$3,250	$4,000	$5,000

Mills Check Boy
1907

Check Boy is a single reeler counter machine very similar to its larger brother, the Dewey. It had a 6 way play feature by which the player could bet from 1 to 6 coins. Winning was a result of putting a coin in the symbol slot that showed up on the reel. The player was paid in trade checks, thus the name Check Boy seemed logical.

POOR	FAIR	GOOD	EXCELLENT
$2,500	$3,300	$4,100	$5,000

Keeney
Steeplechase
circa 1935

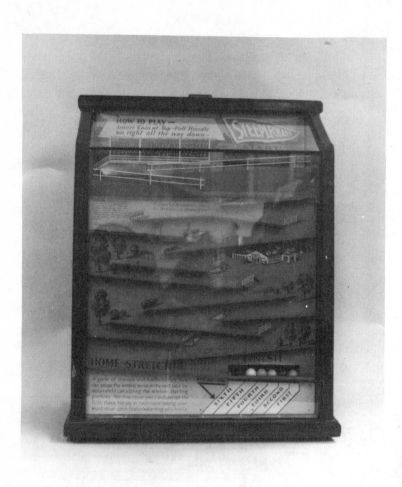

Steeplechase is an exciting horse race game played with marbles.
For a penny, the player can hoist the marbles to the top, and release
them from the starting gate. Up to six competitors could play, betting on different colors to win.

POOR	FAIR	GOOD	EXCELLENT
$250	$330	$410	$500

Rockola
Official Sweepstakes
1933

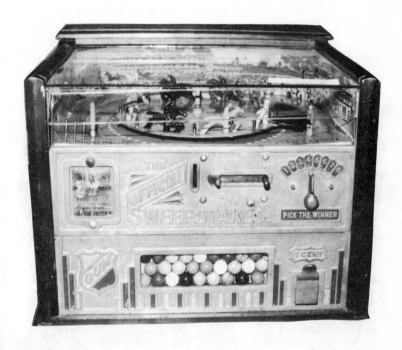

Rockola was thought of as a jukebox company, but they also produced trade stimulators. The player selected a number and gave the handle a push. Figural painted ponies spun around the track, while a ballbearing spun with them to determine the odds. Selecting the right number was a payoff of the odds times the bet wagered.

POOR	FAIR	GOOD	EXCELLENT
$375	$500	$625	$750

Groetchen Punchette
1938

Groetchen played on a radio theme by making their trade stimulator look like a radio receiver. The player inserted a nickel and punched a revolving tape by pulling a handle. The resulting punch was then compared to a radio frequency pay card to determine the payout.

POOR	FAIR	GOOD	EXCELLENT
$300	$400	$500	$600

Fields
Blackjack 21
1931

Notice on the paycard the very strong warning that this machine is not a gambling device: Believe that, and we've got a bridge to sell you. This was simply a game of flipping a ball bearing in the slots to come up to a total of 21 without going over.

POOR	FAIR	GOOD	EXCELLENT
$100	$150	$200	$250

ABT Rol-let
circa 1935

Rol-let looks like a roulette game but it plays like a slot machine. A ball shot into the playing field lands in holes corresponding to slot symbols. There are payoffs according to the appropriate combinations of symbols. ABT was most famous for their coin acceptors that have been used extensively on coin-op machines.

POOR	FAIR	GOOD	EXCELLENT
$225	$300	$375	$450

Buckley Cent-a-Pack
1935

In the 1890's trade stimulators were used to sell cigars, and 40 years later they were being used to sell cigarettes. The game concept of the Cent-a-Pack was simple, and it showed up again and again. The object was to line up 3 of a kind on the reels for cigarette payouts.

POOR	FAIR	GOOD	EXCELLENT
$200	$260	$320	$400

Automatic Games
The Ace
circa 1931

The Ace is the typical trade stimulator of the period. It is based on a 3 reeler slot machine format. The play was very similar to the one arm bandit except winners were paid over the counter, and there was always a consolation prize of a gumball.

POOR	FAIR	GOOD	EXCELLENT
$200	$260	$320	$400

**Caille Fortune
Ball Gum Vendor
1927**

For 1¢ the customer received a gumball and his fortune. The fortune was translated from the paycard according to bell-fruit symbols that had payoffs similar to the 3 reelers that this machine was based on.

POOR	FAIR	GOOD	EXCELLENT
$500	$600	$800	$1,000

**Daval Gum Vendor
1932**

Daval is a cute, simple little machine that has a 3 reeler slot machine format. It vended the inevitable gumball as did almost all of the trade stimulators of the time. The reason, of course, was to stay within the scope of the law. It's interesting to note that these gumballs were often close to inedible. Gumballs were an overhead item, so operators tended to buy the cheapest thing they could find.

POOR	FAIR	GOOD	EXCELLENT
$225	$300	$375	$450

Daval Spin-A-Pack
1935

The first time I saw this machine I did a double take because it looked just like a Daval Win-A-Pack. It should, since they are the same machine; only the marquees are different.

POOR	FAIR	GOOD	EXCELLENT
$150	$200	$250	$300

Daval Reel Dice
1936

Reel Dice was the dice counterpart of the Daval Reel 21. In this game the player spun the reels instead of rolling the dice to make his point.

POOR	FAIR	GOOD	EXCELLENT
$125	$165	$205	$250

**Daval Races
1936**

Daval Races is a kissing cousin to Daval Reel Dice. They were both basically the same cabinet, only featuring a different game theme made obvious by name.

POOR	FAIR	GOOD	EXCELLENT
$150	$190	$230	$275

**Daval
Tit Tat Toe
1936**

Daval offered a large variety of games in the 1930's but this cabinet style seemed to predominate in all of their mid-1930's games. It's different in its game theme, and they don't turn up too often.

POOR	FAIR	GOOD	EXCELLENT
$150	$190	$230	$275

**Daval Tally
1938**

Tally was the typical three-reel cigarette trade stimulator with a little twist. Three numbers showed at the top across from the Tally arrow. If the correct combination of numbers appeared, a jackpot was paid off.

POOR	FAIR	GOOD	EXCELLENT
$150	$200	$250	$300

**Daval Penny Pack
1939**

Daval's Penny Pack is basically the same machine as the Buddy, which was made again in 1946. Since the cigarette 3 reeler was used over and over again, it without a doubt was very popular with the public. It's not surprising, since for 1¢, the customer had a shot at winning from 1 to 10 packs of cigarettes.

POOR	FAIR	GOOD	EXCELLENT
$150	$200	$250	$300

Daval Buddy
1946

The Buddy is representative of the cigarette trade stimulators that were popular in the 1940's. Most everyone would chance a penny for a pack of cigarettes. At the worst, the player was going to get a gumball out of the deal.

POOR	FAIR	GOOD	EXCELLENT
$125	$165	$205	$250

**Daval Freeplay
1946**

Daval played with a pinball machine feature of paying off in free plays. The free plays could be played off, or cancelled, and registered on the inside which meant the customer was paid across the counter. During the late forties, this feature worked fairly well for getting around gambling laws.

POOR	FAIR	GOOD	EXCELLENT
$100	$130	$160	$200

**Groetchen Fortune Teller
1935**

Fortune strips are a familiar con that were used over and over by the gaming industry. The idea, of course, is that the machine only was designed to amuse the customer with a glib fortune printed on the reel strip; and if that wasn't enough, it also vended a gumball. Of course, just for the fun of it, payoffs were shown for certain combinations.

POOR	FAIR	GOOD	EXCELLENT
$225	$300	$375	$450

**Groetchen Dandy Vendor
1932**

Groetchen's Dandy Vendor is a format that was used by many manufacturers. It includes the slot machine, 3 reeler format, and vends a gumball every time. The player could gamble 1¢, 5¢, 10¢ or 25¢ and the last coin played was shown in the little window on the right side. These little windows were used to detect slugs, and to let the shopkeeper know how much was gambled in case of a requested playoff. That's right; there was dishonesty even in the 1930's. The gumball viewing area noted strong warnings against using slugs or foreign coins. This particular model comes with a carousel coin divider that ejects every 4th coin to the operator.

POOR	FAIR	GOOD	EXCELLENT
$250	$330	$410	$500

**Groetchen Penny Smoke
circa 1936**

All of the manufacturers were getting on the cigarette trade stimulator bandwagon. Of course Groetchen was no exception. This aluminum cabinet features nice lines and good graphic appeal.

POOR	FAIR	GOOD	EXCELLENT
$225	$300	$375	$450

Douglis Puritan Baby Vendor
1930

A quick look at this machine would lead most people to think it was a Mills, with the Puritan name on the top, and the 1776 liberty bell on the front. Instead, it was produced by Douglis Novelty. There were a number of Baby Vendors on this theme, and it was not unusual for one manufacturer to copy another.

POOR	FAIR	GOOD	EXCELLENT
$225	$300	$375	$450

Garden City Novelty
Gem
circa 1937

Three reel cigarette trade stimulators were as common in the 1930's and 1940's as pinball machines are today. Grocery stores, service stations, restaurants and any other place operators could think of were markets for small trade stimulators. This machine gave a bonus gumball with every spin of the reels.

POOR	FAIR	GOOD	EXCELLENT
$100	$140	$180	$225

Groetchen
Mercury
1939

There were thousands of these little trade stimulators throughout the country. It was the popular 3 reel slot machine concept using cigarette label symbols. A player lining up 3 of a kind would receive a token good for from 1 to 10 packs of cigarettes.

POOR	FAIR	GOOD	EXCELLENT
$125	$165	$205	$250

Groetchen Tavern
1935

Tavern was dedicated to the drinkers of the world. While most trade stimulators were promoting cigarettes or trade checks, the Tavern was putting money in the pockets of the bar owners. The Tavern is the familiar 3 reel concept with the only difference being the beer and whiskey symbols on the reel strips.

POOR	FAIR	GOOD	EXCELLENT
$225	$300	$375	$450

Mills Puritan
1905

This early trade stimulator resembled a cash register. Was that to make the customer think it was loaded with money, or was it to fool the local lawman? This early model used numbered symbols as opposed to the fruit symbol used on the later Puritan Bell. It was also made in cast iron, whereas the Puritan Bell was cast in aluminum.

POOR	FAIR	GOOD	EXCELLENT
$600	$800	$1,000	$1,200

Groetchen - Yankee
circa 1941

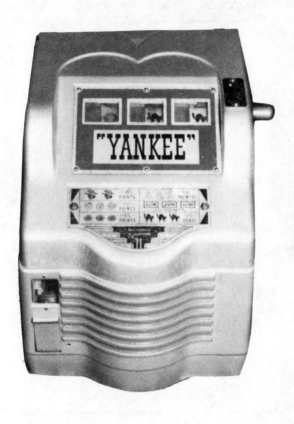

The Yankee is a cute little 3 reeler with basically the same format as a slot machine. Various combinations on 3 reels gave the player points which could be used in trade with the merchant. Of course, a gumball was delivered every time. Groetchen made similar machines called the Poko Reel and Klix.

POOR	FAIR	GOOD	EXCELLENT
$100	$140	$180	$225

Mills Puritan Bell
1926

Mills Puritan was made for a number of years starting in the early 1900's and running through the 1930's. The one shown is the so-called modern version. It resembled a cash register, possibly to escape the eye of a passing law official. The game itself was a 3 reeler just like slots, except the player was paid across the counter.

POOR	FAIR	GOOD	EXCELLENT
$400	$500	$600	$700

**Pierce
Whirlwind
1933**

Whirlwind's art deco case and nice graphic lines make it an attractive machine. One model of the Whirlwind has 3 spinning discs instead of reels, which bears a distinct similarity to the Jennings Little Duke slot machine. The model shown has a visible jackpot that could be released by the operator, for an appropriate winner.

POOR	FAIR	GOOD	EXCELLENT
$350	$450	$550	$650

**Pierce
Whirlwind
(disc model)
1933**

Whirlwind, by Pierce, is unique because of its spinning disc instead of reels. Almost all manufacturers of the time used reels, as did the payout slot machines. The disc set up on the Whirlwind is very similar to the Little Duke slot machine.

POOR	FAIR	GOOD	EXCELLENT
$400	$550	$700	$850

**Superior Cigarette
Ball Gum Vendor
1935**

Superior is the typical ball gum vendor, cigarette reel format of the mid-1930's. Interestingly enough, however, it was only a penny play while most others were 1¢, 5¢, 10¢ and even 25¢ plays. For 1¢, the patron always received a gumball and a shot at free packs of cigarettes.

POOR	FAIR	GOOD	EXCELLENT
$250	$325	$400	$500

**Western Empire
circa 1940**

Trade Stimulators began to lose their inventiveness in the 1940s's, and the Empire is a good example of that. It is the typical three-reeler that helped to promote the sale of cigarettes. Interestingly enough, Empires are fairly uncommon, and they don't show up very often in collections.

POOR	FAIR	GOOD	EXCELLENT
$150	$190	$230	$275

Groetchen Gold Rush
1934

Interesting graphics, and the old West theme make Gold Rush an attractive machine. The reel strip combinations corresponded to fortunes to make the machine seem to be a fortune teller instead of a gambling machine. Note the use of one reel with 2 symbols, and the other reel having just 1 symbol.

POOR	FAIR	GOOD	EXCELLENT
$300	$400	$500	$600

Witney Seven Grand
circa 1939

Witney Seven Grand is a fairly large machine, compared to other trade stimulators of the time. After the bet is placed, and the handle pulled, a bell rings, and the dice are put in motion by the spinning disk they set on. Winners are paid for seven of a kind, down through four of a kind.

POOR	FAIR	GOOD	EXCELLENT
$250	$325	$400	$500

Dealer's Choice
circa 1948

One of the late trade stimulators made by Associated Distributors of Detroit, this game goes back to a theme used by many early manufacturers, in that it shows a 5 card poker hand. The unique feature of this machine is that it uses actual, full-sized playing cards. With each 5 cent play, the cards shuffle a new card into place.

POOR	FAIR	GOOD	EXCELLENT
$50	$65	$80	$100

Decatur Fairest Wheel
style 2 circa 1900

The Fairest Wheel is a classic cigar trade stimulator. The weight of a nickel placed in the top slot set the wheel moving. Landing on a two, which didn't happen often, gave the customer two cigars. Landing on a one returned the patron one cigar for his nickel.

POOR	FAIR	GOOD	EXCELLENT
$500	$675	$850	$1,000

Fey Skill Draw
1932

Although this machine doesn't really fit well in any category, it is generally considered a wheel machine since it has 5 spinning wheels with card symbols on each wheel. The player pulls the handle, and gets a poker hand shown in 5 separate windows. He then holds the cards he wants to keep by pushing down the appropriate buttons. Another pull of the handle completes the draw.

POOR	FAIR	GOOD	EXCELLENT
$375	$435	$500	$550

166

VII. Jukeboxes

Roots for jukeboxes can be found in the coin-operated phonographs of the early 1900's. These coin-ops were nothing more than a phonograph with a coin slot added. At the turn of the century, these devices were a curiosity, and they could be found in arcades throughout the country.

It was really Black American culture that brought the jukebox into vogue. During the 1920's, jazz was beginning to have a groundswell of popularity, especially within the Black community. Conservative White society was dead set against this music, which they considered to be the ranting of heathens. In order to listen to their music, Blacks began to open little juke joints. Since these places were small, and the finances were limited, they were fertile ground for coin-operated record players. Manufacturers and operators began to fill the growing need for coin-operated music machines in the late 1920's, and it was a natural to call them jukeboxes.

Seeburg was one of the first to step into the jukebox market with their 1928 Audiophone. Making use of pneumatics borrowed from their player pianos, Seeburg produced an 8 selection automatic phonograph.

About this same time, Homer Capehart released his automatic phonograph. His phonograph had a larger capacity than Seeburg's, and could play both sides of the record. Capehart was a brilliant businessman, and his future looked bright in the coin-op business. However, business reversals and errors in judgement caused the collapse of his business.

The Wurlitzer family, who had been in the music business for years, began to recognize the potential of the coin-operated phonograph business in the early 1930's. They did two things that would make them the kings of the industry. The first was to hire Homer Capehart, who ran their marketing department, and set up dealerships all over the country. The second, was the later addition of Paul Fuller, whose design leadership in the 1940's produced the most beautiful jukeboxes ever made.

Rockola also joined the growing jukebox market in the 1930's. Rockola was actually the owner's last name, not a play on the term rock 'n roll which hadn't even been inspired at that time. Unlike Seeburg and Wurlitzer, Rockola didn't have a background in automated musical instruments. His company produced scales, pinballs, and counter games. However, in the mid-1930's, he recognized the growing market for jukeboxes, and joined the competition.

Other manufacturers jumped on the bandwagon, including Mills, Gabel, AMI, and Filben. In the mid-1930's, the American public recognized the jukebox as an important source of entertainment. Nickels added up to a multimillion dollar industry.

The Golden period of the jukebox was the 1940's. In the spirit of competition, the various manufacturers tried to outdo each other with machines that were more attractive. The result was the most beautiful jukeboxes that were ever produced. Wurlitzer was king in that respect, producing one beautiful model after another. This is the main reason Wurlitzers of the 1940's are the most sought after jukeboxes by collectors.

In the 1950's, the jukebox became the temple of rock 'n roll. Teenagers of this era shaped a new market. The rich woods, and subtle plastics of the 1940's were passe. Their culture commanded brighter chromed boxes, with fins, and outrageous lines. The 78 record was decided to be outdated and cumbersome. It was replaced with the faster, more compact 45's. More selections were required for the wide variety of music that was now available. The jukebox was tied to the hangout, and a general rebellion of adult values.

For the collector this is a sad state of affairs, since jukeboxes of this period have less classic charm. However, jukeboxes of this period are classics in their own right. There is a growing interest in jukeboxes of this era; especially considering the greater availability, and lower cost of these later machines.

In the 1960's the American public began to end their love affair with the jukebox. Many things brought this on; again the rebellious youths of the 1960's rejected traditional values. The Hangout was out, and the sit in was in. A single play on a jukebox was expensive, and many people preferred to invest in an L.P. Superior sound systems became available for home use that outperformed the jukebox as a source of entertainment. Live music regained great popularity in the 1960's. Teenagers preferred listening and dancing to the local 3-piece rock bands that were springing up everywhere.

This trend has continued into the 1970's, and '80's. As a result, the jukebox is becoming extinct. Most people can't remember the last time they played a tune on a jukebox. They are absent from most modern restaurants, and bars, and people don't seem to miss them; or do they?

JUKEBOX INDEX

A M I Model A
1946

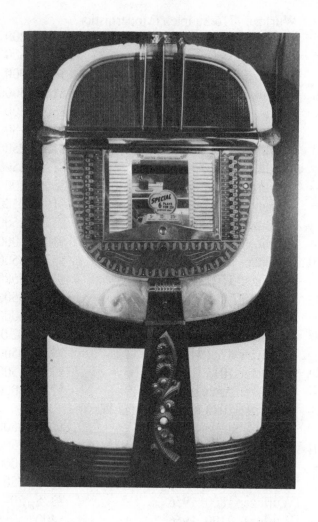

"My God, what is that!" is what can often be heard from people who see an AMI Model A for the first time. This overgrown jukebox has been nicknammed the Mother of Plastic because of the huge mass of plastic used on its colorful front.

POOR	FAIR	GOOD	EXCELLENT
$2,500	$2,800	$3,100	$3,500

Capehart 28-G
circa 1928

Capehart's 28-G sported an 18 play mechanism. There was no selection; the 18 records played in sequence, and then flipped over to play the other side. Homer Capehart, who founded the company, was later a huge force in the Wurlitzer sales organization.

POOR	FAIR	GOOD	EXCELLENT
$1,750	$2,350	$2,950	$3,500

**Mills Carousel
circa 1934**

This jukebox looks a little unusual to the uninitiated. Records are swung on a rotating contraption that does resemble a circus carousel. Twelve selections were available on this massive wood cabinet box.

POOR	FAIR	GOOD	EXCELLENT
$400	$530	$660	$800

**Mills Throne of Music
1939**

Mills Jukeboxes seem to have a streamlined, almost space-age look. Of course, they were born during the century of progress when high technology was beginning to gain momentum. Maybe that's why the ornate and gay Wurlitzers are more popular with collectors.

POOR	FAIR	GOOD	EXCELLENT
$1,200	$1,400	$1,600	$1,800

**Packard Manhattan
1946**

Packard Manhattan was created by Homer Capehart. Homer Capehart was a legend in the jukebox industry, working with Rockola, Wurlitzer, and his own Capehart Company at various times. The Manhattan is a huge 20 selection jukebox. Interestingly enough, many of the internal parts are very similar to Wurlitzers.

POOR	FAIR	GOOD	EXCELLENT
$1,750	$2,350	$2,950	$3,500

**Ristocrat
circa 1952**

This has to be one of the simplest jukeboxes of all time. For 5¢ the patron got to hear a 45 rpm record blare through the tiny amplifier. There was one catch: There was no selection available on the record.

POOR	FAIR	GOOD	EXCELLENT
$100	$125	$150	$175

Rockola 39A Counter Model
1939

This 12 selection Rockola counter model was made for locations with limited space. There was no internal speaker, so it always needed to be hooked up with a remote system. Later models came with a stand that incorporated the speaker. Since these counter model jukeboxes were so small, internal mechanisms were necessarily quite simple.

POOR	FAIR	GOOD	EXCELLENT
$700	$800	$900	$1,000

Model 1422 - Rockola
1946

In terms of jukeboxes recognized by the general public as classics, the Rockola 1422 is probably only second to the Wurlitzer 1015. The classic lines of the 1422 were repeated in the 1426 which was brought out the following year. A revolving color cylinder, fully visible record changer, and a 20 selection multiselector were features that also appeared on the Wurlitzer models.

POOR	FAIR	GOOD	EXCELLENT
$1,200	$1,700	$2,200	$2,800

Rockola 1428
1948

This was the last of Rockola's classic, older style boxes. They, like all of the other manufacturers, left the rounded lines, ornate trim, and beautiful woodwork behind. All Rockolas that followed this one had more modern styling.

POOR	FAIR	GOOD	EXCELLENT
$1,100	$1,500	$1,900	$2,200

Rockola 1448
1955

Is that a 1956 Oldsmobile, or a '55 Rockola? It appears that car manufacturers, and jukebox designers went to the same schools in the 1950's. Fins and chrome were the hallmark of 1950's jukeboxes. Fidelity was greatly improved on this Rockola, as were the selector capabilities.

POOR	FAIR	GOOD	EXCELLENT
$375	$500	$625	$750

Scopitone
1962

Scopitone stands by itself as a unique jukebox, and a marketing mistake. For a fairly hefty 25¢ (other jukeboxes of the period were 10¢ for 1 play, or 3 plays for a quarter) the patron got not only the music, but a film of the recording artist synchronized to the music. The films were produced in France, and they were fairly risque for the time. Unfortunately, film production costs were extremely high, and they quickly disappeared from the scene.

POOR	FAIR	GOOD	EXCELLENT
$1,200	$1,600	$2,000	$2,500

Seeburg Audiphone
1928

The Regular Audiphone is essentially the same as the Audiphone Jr., except it has a larger cabinet. Seeburg adapted their model K, E Roll piano cabinet to produce this very early jukebox. Seeburg was always an innovator, and they realized in advance the potential of a coin-operated record player.

POOR	FAIR	GOOD	EXCELLENT
$1,750	$2,350	$2,950	$3,500

Audiphone Jr. - Seeburg
1928

One of the earliest jukeboxes was the Seeburg Audiphone. It had
8 selections operated by pneumatics borrowed from the player piano.
The familiar coin slide is there, but it could only swallow one nickel
at a time.

POOR	FAIR	GOOD	EXCELLENT
$1,750	$2,350	$2,950	$3,500

Seeburg Symphonola
1935

At first glance, this Seeburg looks like an early floor model radio. The selector even looks like a radio dial. The early symphonola mechanism was a 12 selection system that moved the record over in a tray that was picked up by the turntable.

POOR	FAIR	GOOD	EXCELLENT
$750	$1,000	$1,250	$1,500

Seeburg 8800
1942

The designers at Seeburg must have had a secret fantasy to work in science fiction movies. This 8800 combines the use of beautiful woods and colorful molded plastics just like its Wurlitzer counterpart. Somehow the overall effect is just not the same.

POOR	FAIR	GOOD	EXCELLENT
$900	$1,200	$1,500	$1,800

Seeburg 147
1947

We tried to include this in the last book but the available photograph just was too bad to give any kind of recognition. Well, here it is in all its glory. This jukebox is lovingly called the trashcan. Many collectors hate them, although people who have them really appreciate their classic look. Please note that the one shown has velvet replacing the original ornate metal grillwork.

POOR	FAIR	GOOD	EXCELLENT
$600	$730	$860	$1,000

Seeburg 100 B
1950

Seeburg was often a leader, as was the case with the 100 B. It was the first 45 rpm - only machine on the market. It followed right behind another first, which was the 100 selection 100 A, 78 rpm machine. That was 4 times more choice of selections than the other machines on the market.

POOR	FAIR	GOOD	EXCELLENT
$500	$600	$700	$800

Western Electric Selectraphone
1928

Western Electric was owned by Seeburg in 1928, and the Selectraphone is essentially the same as the Seeburg Audiphone. The record selector mechanism was driven by pneumatics, as in player pianos. This jukebox was essentially all mechanical except for the lights, and the amplifier. The Selectraphone would be considered rarer than the Audiphones.

POOR	FAIR	GOOD	EXCELLENT
$2,000	$2,600	$3,200	$4,000

Wurlitzer P12
1935

P12 is one of Wurlitzer's earliest entries into the jukebox market. The cabinet is very similar to radio cabinets of the period with a coin mechanism added on. Note the 12 choice simplex selector.

POOR	FAIR	GOOD	EXCELLENT
$750	$1,000	$1,250	$1,500

Wurlitzer 24
1937

The model number was significant in that it indicated the number of selections. This was Wurlitzer's first 24 selection machine with their rotary multi-selector. These machines are in short supply because many were dismantled to make rotary Victories.

POOR	FAIR	GOOD	EXCELLENT
$1,500	$2,000	$2,500	$3,000

Model 800 Wurlitzer
1940

In the year 1940, Wurlitzer was prolific in its production of jukeboxes. They produced eleven new models under the excellent design leadership of Paul Fuller. Over 11,000 of the model 800 were produced. The inside mechanism for the Wurlitzers was essentially the same. All models featured a 20 selection multiselector, and a visible turntable system. The model shown is in unrestored condition.

POOR	FAIR	GOOD	EXCELLENT
$1,750	$2,350	$2,950	$3,500

Wurlitzer Model 500
circa 1938

The model 500 was a successful jukebox for Wurlitzer, and they continued production on it for several years. While not as showy as later models, it has the classic Wurlitzer charm. Notice the more liberal use of colorful plastics; that was a sign of things to come.

POOR	FAIR	GOOD	EXCELLENT
$1,250	$1,650	$2,050	$2,500

Wurlitzer 600
1938

The model 600 was produced for several years by Wurlitzer, and proved a success for them. It employed the use of a rotary selector that was unique to Wurlitzer. It's interesting to note that the record cabinet look started to change at this time into a more flashy, attention-getting machine. This model was also available with keyboard selector.

POOR	FAIR	GOOD	EXCELLENT
$1,250	$1,650	$2,050	$2,500

Counter Model 71 - Wurlitzer
1940

Wurlitzer's advertising campaign suggested such obscure locations as barbeque stands, excursion boats, and filling stations as good prospects for a counter model. The model pictured shows the matching stand with its beautiful wood, and graphics work.

POOR	FAIR	GOOD	EXCELLENT
$1,500	$2,000	$2,500	$3,500

Stand

$500	$1,000	$1,500	$2,000

Wurlitzer 750
1941

Another of Paul Fuller's great design classics. It's hard to believe that one designer could have produced so many great jukeboxes in one year. The 750 was just one of the many different classics that rolled out of Wurlitzer's factory in 1940.

POOR	FAIR	GOOD	EXCELLENT
$1,750	$2,350	$2,950	$3,500

780 Wurlitzer
1941

The 780 is better known as The Colonial. It was designed for the location that wanted a more conservative appeal. The Wurlitzer sales literature described it as a masterpiece, rich in old world charm.

POOR	FAIR	GOOD	EXCELLENT
$1,750	$2,350	$2,950	$3,500

Model 850 Wurlitzer
1941

Better known as The Peacock, the Wurlitzer 850 was a Paul Fuller - designed classic. Fuller was prolific in his creation of unique and beautiful Wurlitzers. Approximately 10,500 of these machines were manufactured and they were eagerly sought after by operators. The Peacock is still eagerly sought after by collectors all over the world.

POOR	FAIR	GOOD	EXCELLENT
$3,000	$4,000	$5,000	$6,000

Wurlitzer Model 950
1942

King of Kings is the only way to describe the Wurlitzer 950. Two things make this jukebox the most coveted by collectors in general. One is rarity, due to the fact that less than 3500 were delivered from the factory. The second reason is the beautiful overall appearance.

POOR	FAIR	GOOD	EXCELLENT
$6,000	$8,000	$10,000	$12,000

Wurlitzer Model 42
Victory
1942

If Wurlitzer's model 950 is the king of collectible jukeboxes, the Victory has to be the queen. This machine was put together with more or less spare parts since raw materials were being used for the war effort. Rarity and beauty equal desirability and that sums it up for the Victory.

POOR	FAIR	GOOD	EXCELLENT
$3,250	$4,250	$5,250	$6,500

Wurlitzer 1015
1946

Wurlitzer 1015 is probably the classic of classic jukeboxes. When Hollywood wants a showy jukebox, they usually call on the 1015's for their models. At the end of the War, Wurlitzer pulled out all of the stops, and told Paul Fuller to give it his best shot. The result was the 1015, and it was the most successful jukebox of all time.

POOR	FAIR	GOOD	EXCELLENT
$2,500	$3,500	$4,500	$5,500

Model 1080 Wurlitzer
1947

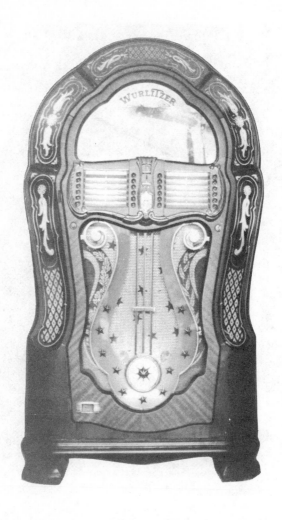

Paul Fuller designed the 1080 with more conservative establishments in mind. Beautifully mirrored graphics replaced the color wheels and bubbler tubes of the 1015. 1015's outsold the 1080, seven to one.

POOR	FAIR	GOOD	EXCELLENT
$2,500	$3,500	$4,500	$5,500

Model 1100 - Wurlitzer
1948

The Space Age design of the 1100 was a sign of the times. Post war America had the dream of a modern, streamlined new era. The 1100 was the last Wurlitzer produced under the design leadership of Paul Fuller. Bubbler tubes, fancy metal castings, richly colored plastics, and beautiful wood inlays were sadly absent from this model. Although the 1100 is a beautiful machine in its own right, it sadly marked the end of an era.

POOR	FAIR	GOOD	EXCELLENT
$1,250	$1,600	$2,000	$2,500

Wurlitzer 1800
circa 1956

It's interesting that when most people think back to the Rock and Roll era, they think of classic jukeboxes like the 1015. Actually the classic jukeboxes were pre-rock and roll. More modern looking machines with streamlined lines characterized the Rock and Roll era. The 1800 is not a classic in terms of styling, yet it is an excellent representative of the heyday of rock and roll. One hundred and four record selections were available and that pleased the operators and the patrons.

POOR	FAIR	GOOD	EXCELLENT
$375	$500	$625	$750

Wurlitzer 1050
1973

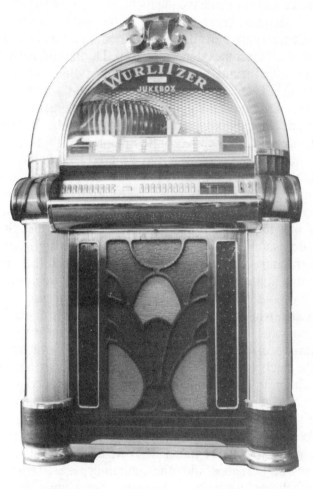

The 1050 was Wurlitzer's last ditch effort before going out of the jukebox business. It was the company's hope that a nostalgia-evoking machine would help pump resources back into the company's treasury. Unfortunately, the 1050 was not enough, and the company's jukebox division finally gave up. Like many artists who never live to see their work appreciated, the 1050 is now in great demand by collectors.

POOR	FAIR	GOOD	EXCELLENT
$2,500	$3,300	$4,100	$5,000

IX. Arcade and Amusement Machines

Arcade and amusement equipment, like most of the other coin-operated machines, began to appear in significant numbers in the 1890's. Centers called arcades were started, that housed a number of amusement machines under one roof. During this early period they were called penny arcades because everything was operated by a penny. These arcades experienced great success because Americans were apparently hungry for entertainment.

Arcades quickly began to fill up with a number of entertainment devices. Edison's coin-operated phonograph was a favorite. For 1¢ the customer could listen to a prerecorded musical performance. Drop card machines showed exotic, faraway places, disasters, and erotic peeks at naughty ladies. Flip card machines, a product of Mutoscope, gave the illusion of motion. Lung testers tested the patrons' blowing capacity, and registered it on a big dial. Strength testers used spring tension to register a customer's grip strength. Illusion machines, and fortune tellers gently conned the player by offering him mystical information. Electrical shock treatments were sold with various inducements; some offered medical cures for multiple ailments, while others were endurance tests. Iron claws were all time favorites. The player tried to maneuver a crane with a hinged scoop into place, scoop up a prize, and deposit it in the reward chute. Often the bucket had a tendency to spill before making it to the reward chute. In spite of the pitfalls, people still kept coming back for more. Orchestrians were also popular, offering the entertainment of what sounded like a marching band.

Arcades were not the only places where amusement games and arcade equipment could be found. They were also present in saloons, poolrooms, barber shops, and other gathering places. These amusement machines were the common American's source of entertainment.

During the 1930's, pinball games started to become popular. The term pinball came from the metal posts, or pins, that the ball dodged through. Early pin games were much smaller than their modern counterparts, and they did not have flippers. The only real control the player had was in how hard he fired the ball. The scoring holes were numbered, and by a manual count, the total score was determined.

Pinball games are significant for one important reason: Pinballs are the only amusement game whose popularity has endured into the present time. Many arcade owners didn't include pinballs in their inventory because they wanted to maintain a family atmosphere. As things progressed in the 1930's, however, it was mostly the so-called less desirable types that were frequenting arcades.

Arcades began to disappear in the late 1930's. The ones that were left in the 1940's and 1950's were most connected with amusement parks. The motion picture show had taken over as the entertainment medium of the masses. Eventually, most of the classic amusement games lost popularity to the pinballs.

The interest in pinball games is at an all-time high today. Arcades have resurfaced with electronic marvels made possible through silicone chips. While pinballs are still as popular as ever, they are being joined by a host of video games whose game themes have endless possibilities. Although the games and their technology have changed, playful Americans are still willing to part with their pocket change for fun.

Arcade machines have been organized in this edition according to type. For example, shocker, grip, skill machines, etc. have been listed under their appropriate categories. Sometimes machines could be listed in several different categories; the attempt, however, has been to list each machine under the most logical heading.

ARCADE MACHINE INDEX

Bingo
1931

Bingo was one of the earliest pin games. It was produced by several manufacturers, including Bingo novelty, Gottlieb, and Field.

POOR	FAIR	GOOD	EXCELLENT
$250	$325	$400	$500

Booz Barometer
circa 1950

A late arcade game that has an obvious relationship to drinking establishments. The idea is to start at one end with the handle and move it to the other end without touching the ring to the rod. Failing at this test sets off lights and buzzers.

POOR	FAIR	GOOD	EXCELLENT
$75	$100	$125	$150

Challenger Duckshoot
circa 1940

One of the simplest arcade machines ever produced was the Challenger. Put in a penny into a mechanical gun; then try to shoot the duck. Very simply, it was a poor man's shooting gallery.

POOR	FAIR	GOOD	EXCELLENT
$125	$165	$205	$250

Chester Pollard
Play the Derby
circa 1930

Chester Pollard games were popular in arcades. They were set up so that two people could compete against each other. In the Derby, each player turned his wheel to move his horse. The horse raced around an oval track, and the first one across the finish line was the winner.

POOR	FAIR	GOOD	EXCELLENT
$1,500	$2,000	$2,500	$3,000

Exhibit Supply Novelty Merchantman
circa 1942

Claw machines have always been a favorite in arcades. Put a coin in and the shovel could be directed to a prize. If the player was lucky, and they usually weren't, they would grab the prize they wanted, and direct it back over to the chute. Exhibit Supply sold this model in large numbers.

POOR	FAIR	GOOD	EXCELLENT
$600	$800	$1,000	$1,200

Fey Shoot The Ducks
1928

Charles Fey, of slot machine fame, was a great tinkerer. He dabbled in most types of coin-operated machines, and Shoot the Ducks was one of his ventures into the arcade field. If the trigger was pressed at the same time as the duck was passing over the appropriate contact point, the duck fell backward, giving the illusion of being hit by a bullet. The example shown, which is the only one known to exist, is under restoration.

RARE

Gottlieb Whizz Bang
1932

Gottlieb was into the pinball game business very early, and his success continued for a number of years. Whizz Bang offered a brightly colored playing field, with the usual pin obstacles, and the numbered drop holes.

POOR	FAIR	GOOD	EXCELLENT
$250	$325	$400	$500

Chester Pollard
Play Football
circa 1925

Just about everyone remembers seeing a Chester Pollard game at one time or another, and just about everyone likes them. They have a very classic look, and they're fun to play.

POOR	FAIR	GOOD	EXCELLENT
$1,000	$1,300	$1,600	$2,000

Groetchen
Pike's Peak
1940

Is it an arcade game or a trade stimulator? According to the original company advertising, it's a counter skill game with unlimited play possibilities, whatever that means. It came in 1¢ and 5¢ models, and the idea was to walk a ballbearing up the incline by skillful use of the knob.

POOR	FAIR	GOOD	EXCELLENT
$125	$165	$205	$250

Gottlieb's Big Broadcast
1933

Gottlieb was one of the front runners in the pinball industry. Coin-operated entertainment was becoming big business, and Gottlieb was prolific in the production of pinball games. Big Broadcast was one of his very successful early pins that played on the radio broadcasting theme.

POOR	FAIR	GOOD	EXCELLENT
$250	$325	$400	$500

Gottlieb 4 Belles
1954

Four Belles is one of Gottlieb's early flipper games. Flipper games added a whole new dimension in pinballs. Flippers made the element of skill much more important. Notice the interesting lithography of the back glass.

POOR	FAIR	GOOD	EXCELLENT
$250	$325	$400	$500

Gottlieb's Gold Star
1954

Gottlieb's Gold Star falls in the oak rail, early flipper game era. Kids growing up in the 1950's remember these games well. Most would rather play one of these simple games over the highly sophisticated, electronic marvels of today. Pretty girls are predominant on the back glass of this game, and they were a recurring theme on most games up through the present.

POOR	FAIR	GOOD	EXCELLENT
$200	$250	$300	$450

Keeney's League Leader
1951

Keeney was one of the smaller pinball manufacturers. In this popular game the player pushed the button to release the ball and with the other button he swung a bat. The hit balls flew into various tiers, scoring hits, runs, or outs.

POOR	FAIR	GOOD	EXCELLENT
$250	$325	$400	$500

Mills Owl
1942

Mills was mostly devoted to the production of slot machines, but surprisingly enough they did dabble in the pinball market. The back glass of this pinball does have a definite similarity to a slot machine, and this model was produced in both payout, and non-payout types.

POOR	FAIR	GOOD	EXCELLENT
$300	$400	$500	$600

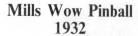
Mills Wow Pinball
1932

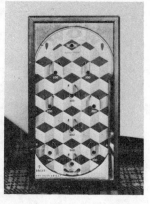

Psychedelic must have started in 1932, because that's what the Wow color scheme looked like. It was definitely an eyecatcher which must have been the secret of its success. The mechanics of the game are a lot less exciting than the color scheme.

POOR	FAIR	GOOD	EXCELLENT
$235	$315	$395	$475

Rockola
World Series
1937

Simulated baseball is always hard to pass up. This Rockola plays like the real game. The player tries to hit the baseball controlled by a lever on the front of the machine. Balls, strikes, and outs are scored, and play continues until three outs are logged. Each one of the metal players displays a name of the corresponding player who was in the World Series.

POOR	FAIR	GOOD	EXCELLENT
$600	$800	$1,000	$1,200

Mutoscope It's A Knockout
circa 1941

It's a Knockout is an exciting, two player action game. Players on each side of the machine maneuver a control handle. The object is to have your boxer punch the other boxer on the chin, and score a knockout.

POOR	FAIR	GOOD	EXCELLENT
$550	$730	$910	$1,100

Radio Station
circa 1933

In the early days of pinball, there were no flippers, and automatic scoring devices. The games were basically mechanical and it was a score-it-yourself system. Gambling was often associated with pin-balls, and for that reason, they were later made illegal in certain states. Radio station was a bright, inviting game that played on the radio theme which was in its heyday.

POOR	FAIR	GOOD	EXCELLENT
$250	$325	$400	$500

Seeburg
Chicken Sam
circa 1931

Shooting galleries are arcade classics, and they are still popular with arcade patrons. Seeburg's Chicken Sam character adds a little more amusement and pizzaz to this shoot 'em up game.

POOR	FAIR	GOOD	EXCELLENT
$500	$660	$820	$1,000

Stephens
Babe Ruth Baseball
circa 1935

Babe Ruth Baseball was created by Stephen's Novelty Company of Milwaukee. The object of the game was to move the baseball player into position, and catch the ballbearing falling through the player field. Catching all 5 balls gave the highest score possible.

POOR	FAIR	GOOD	EXCELLENT
$300	$400	$500	$600

228

Midland
Electricity is Life
circa 1902

Why would an electric shock treatment be popular at an arcade? In the early part of the century, electricity held a certain magic quality. Uses for electricity were still being discovered. Also note the challenge on the front of the machine: Who can hold the most?

POOR	FAIR	GOOD	EXCELLENT
$1,000	$1,300	$1,600	$2,000

Williams Peppy The Clown
circa 1950

It's seldom that something really different comes along. Peppy the Clown is a unique exception. For some pocket change, Peppy dances and sings. The customer gets to push four buttons that control the clown like a marionette.

POOR	FAIR	GOOD	EXCELLENT
$325	$465	$605	$750

Medina Mfg. Spirometer
circa 1911

This unusual arcade device was both a lung tester and an electric shock treatment machine. These machines could also be found in doctor's offices and pharmacies because an electric shock was believed to have medicinal qualities. Imagine how healthful it would be to use the lung tester mouthpiece right behind a guy who had typhoid.

POOR	FAIR	GOOD	EXCELLENT
$750	$1,000	$1,250	$1,500

Caille Cail-o-scope
circa 1905

Viewers were very popular in arcades. This Caille was the dropcard type which slowly dropped one three dimensional view at a time. The views told a mini-story featuring comedies, tragedies, and sex.

POOR	FAIR	GOOD	EXCELLENT
$1,000	$1,300	$1,600	$2,000

Exhibit Supply Viewer
circa 1935

Exhibit Supply was probably the largest maker of countertop machines. Part of the reason for this was their carnival and traveling show market. These people were on the move, and compact, money making machines were right up their alley. The machine pictured offers a sexy show and that was also very popular with the carneys.

POOR	FAIR	GOOD	EXCELLENT
$200	$260	$320	$400

Caille Happy Home
circa 1910

This early peep show is very unique. For one penny, the shutter on the front of the house raised, and the viewer was treated to a 3 dimensional view of a lady preparing for bed.

POOR	FAIR	GOOD	EXCELLENT
$600	$800	$1,000	$1,200

Mutoscope (Clam Shell)
circa 1895

The Mutoscope gave the viewer the closest thing to a moving picture available at that time. A series of pictures showing different positions in a scene flipped in sequence, giving the illusion of motion. There were comedies, disasters, and so-called art studies.

POOR	FAIR	GOOD	EXCELLENT
$900	$1,100	$1,400	$1,800

Mills Quartoscope
circa 1900

Mills outdid Caille this time on cabinet style and general eye appeal. This drop card machine operates in a similar manner to the Caille Cail-o-scope. There is more gingerbread on the cabinet, and an interesting casting of an almost naked lady near the eyepiece.

POOR	FAIR	GOOD	EXCELLENT
$1,100	$1,460	$1,820	$2,250

Exhibit Supply
Sex Appeal Meter
circa 1930

This machine very clearly displays the ESCO decal that of course was an abbreviation for Exhibit Supply Company. It's hard to believe that this concept ever took in much money. However, for the time, it was slightly risque and could be amusing for a young fellow and his date.

POOR	FAIR	GOOD	EXCELLENT
$400	$530	$660	$800

**Mutoscope
Tin Model
1940**

In the spirit of American manufacturing philosophy, Mutoscope wanted to make their machine for less money. Therefore, they changed from the beautiful, ornate, heavy cast iron machines, to the simplified straight line, tin machines. After all, the customer put his penny in for the show, not the quality of the machine. The internal mechanism, and flip card concept were essentially the same as the earlier Clam Shell model.

POOR	FAIR	GOOD	EXCELLENT
300	$400	$500	$600

**Exhibit Supply
Striking Clock
circa 1930**

Striking Clock was a unique concept in strength testers. The harder the squeeze, the farther the dial would register; which was typical of all strength testers. However, this one sounded the bell like a striking clock, to let every one in the arcade know how well the participant had done.

POOR	FAIR	GOOD	EXCELLENT
$750	$1,000	$1,250	$1,500

**Exhibit Supply
Kiss-o-Meter
circa 1930**

Exhibit Supply often employed rather suggestive themes; imagine the teenagers back in the 1940's plopping their money in, and giggling at the results.

POOR	FAIR	GOOD	EXCELLENT
$250	$330	$410	$500

**Gatter Novelty
Grip Tester
circa 1925**

This grip tester came in a nice oak cabinet with cast claw feet. The grip test itself was pretty much the same format as all of the other grip testers on the market. A pull all the way to the top rang the bell.

POOR	FAIR	GOOD	EXCELLENT
$1,000	$1,300	$1,600	$2,000

Mutoscope Punch a Bag
circa 1910

What a great way to get rid of aggression and help to pay some operator's bills. After inserting a coin, the bag was pulled back towards the customer. The puncher then let go with his best shot which registered on the Punch a Bag meter.

POOR	FAIR	GOOD	EXCELLENT
$900	$1,130	$1,360	$1,600

Cupid's Post Office
circa 1935

Cupid's Post Office is a sort of lonely heart's club for the person of small means. For 5¢ (later updated to 10¢) the patron received a letter appropriately addressed to gents or ladies. The letters were flowery, and filled with endearments of love.

POOR	FAIR	GOOD	EXCELLENT
$700	$930	$1,160	$1,400

Exhibit Supply
Model E Card Vendor
circa 1925

The original Exhibit Supply catalogue describes as follows: "This is a standard machine for portable arcades made with quickly detachable top frame, especially for carnivals". The top frame was so detachable that they are hardly ever found with the machine. Exhibit Supply Company felt that every carnival arcade should have at least 16 of these machines.

POOR	FAIR	GOOD	EXCELLENT
$150	$200	$250	$300

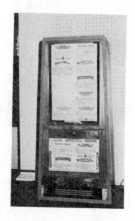

Exhibit Supply Card Vendor
circa 1935

Exhibit Supply was heavily into the card vending business. This way the arcade customer received something tangible for his money. This particular machine gives the patron a diploma.

POOR	FAIR	GOOD	EXCELLENT
$125	$165	$205	$250

**Exhibit Supply
Oracle Fortune Teller
circa 1925**

In the original catalogue the oracle is described as follows: "The Oracle is the greatest little fortune teller machine ever made—a special feature is its winning appearance—bright colored appealing signs and natural finished oak cabinet. The Oracle answers all sorts of comic and serious questions as shown on the dial."

POOR	FAIR	GOOD	EXCELLENT
$150	$200	$250	$300

**Mutoscope Love Teller
circa 1935**

Put your palm on the handspring and the machine tells your love capacity. Patrons are often concerned that these machines are shockers, although this one isn't.

POOR	FAIR	GOOD	EXCELLENT
$300	$400	$500	$600

Exhibit Supply
Mystic Eye
circa 1935

Mystic Eye is very large and imposing considering its rather simple task of delivering a printed fortune card. Its sheet metal exterior doesn't do much in the esthetics department.

POOR	FAIR	GOOD	EXCELLENT
$300	$400	$500	$600

Jennings Comet
circa 1930

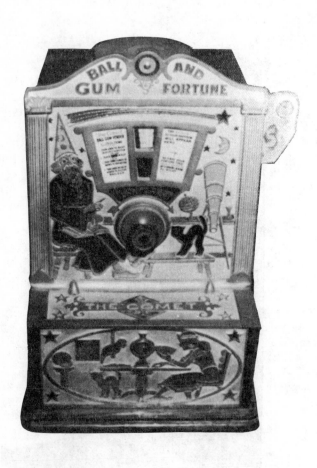

The Comet is Jenning's version of a fortune telling machine, somewhat patterned after Mills' Wizard. For 1¢ the patron asked a question, turned a dial, was given an answer, and a gumball. Notice the wizard and the fortune teller cast on the front.

POOR	FAIR	GOOD	EXCELLENT
$400	$530	$660	$800

Mills Wizard Fortune Teller
circa 1920

What's my fortune? Put in a penny, select one of 6 questions, and give the fortune wheel a spin. The resulting fortunes were more humorous than they were mystical.

POOR	FAIR	GOOD	EXCELLENT
$300	$400	$500	$600

Cremona Style K Orchestrian
circa 1908

This beautiful upright orchestrian featured eight instruments. For 5¢ the client was entertained with the next tune on the roll. As the holes on the roll passed by a tube, a pneumatic was collapsed, and a corresponding instrument played. What an ingenious way to make music.

POOR	FAIR	GOOD	EXCELLENT
$15,000	$20,000	$25,000	$30,000

Mills Violano Virtuoso
circa 1912

This amazing musical entertainment machine was a combination violin and piano concert. A perforated paper roll allowed wires on either side to make contact at the appropriate time and perform the functions of the machine. There was a transformer that converted electrical current to D.C. Violano was heralded as one of the mechanical marvels of the time.

POOR	FAIR	GOOD	EXCELLENT
$8,000	$10,500	$13,000	$16,000

27" Regina Upright
Style 8A Changer
1896

This beautiful music box was a forerunner to the jukebox. The selector knob allowed for 12 different selections of the huge metal disks that were lifted into the upper cabinet by the changer. Two ornately carved dragons stood guard over the glass viewing window.

POOR	FAIR	GOOD	EXCELLENT
$7,500	$10,000	$12,500	$15,000

X. Vending Machines

Vending machines began to become popular in America in the later 1800's. Automation was beginning to appear everywhere, and the concept of an automatic clerk was a natural. The advantages of these contraptions were obvious. The machines were always on duty, they collected no wage, and face to face contact with the public was unnecessary.

The most common product vended was gum. It came in sticks of various sizes, rectangular blobs called tabs, and brightly colored gum balls. In the early machines of the 1890's, through 1910, wrapped sticks and tab gum seemed to be the most prevalent. One of the favorites of the time was Adams, with their famous tutti-fruitti. There were a number of others, such as Zeno, Colgans, and Mansfield, all of which have disappeared over the years. It's interesting to note that this marketing concept had a huge percentage of the country chewing gum, a habit which disgusted Europeans.

The popularity of vending gum through a machine made way for vending a number of other products through machines. Cigars were a popular product of the times. Many men felt that it was masculine, and successful-looking to smoke cigars. Various cigar vendors began to appear, incorporating their own cigar cutters. Of course, since the customer now has a cigar, he needs a match to light it with. Inevitably, match vendors were popular. It's peculiar that matches were sold in the 1890's, and they are given away in the 1980's.

Another convenience product that was vended early in the century was collar buttons. Collar buttons were used to attach detachable collars on men's shirts. Detachable collars made it possible to have a clean collar, without laundering the whole shirt. Unfortunately, collar buttons were small, and easily lost, so the collar vendor served a need.

Over the years, machine manufacturers have produced vendors for almost everything imaginable. The vendors knew that in order to sell their products, the machine and product needed to attract the customer's attention. Many of the machines were beautifully ornate, and brightly painted. Some had animated figures that entertained the customer while he or she received the product. Many had mechanisms that were fascinating to watch. The result, of course, were some incredibly beautiful machines that are unique works of art. Unfortunately over the years, the ornate machines have given way to more streamlined, no-nonsense vendors that aren't much fun. However, there seems to be no slowdown of the American public's willingness to buy products from a machine.

VENDING MACHINE INDEX

249

Exhibit Supply Company - Card Vendor
circa 1930

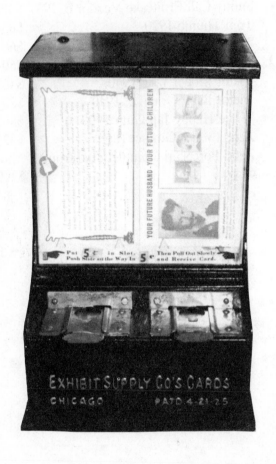

This card machine was set up to vend novelty cards. The particular one shown vends a card showing your future husband or wife, and children. If that idea doesn't appeal to the customer, there's a lonely hearts club card.

POOR	FAIR	GOOD	EXCELLENT
$75	$100	$125	$150

Ohio Book Matches Dispenser
circa 1950

This match book vendor was a simple little device that was prevalent in restaurants, smoke shops, pool rooms, etc. The ornate castings and glass viewing areas that were part of earlier match vendors, are conspiciously absent in this vendor.

POOR	FAIR	GOOD	EXCELLENT
$20	$30	$40	$50

Abbey Gum Vendor
circa 1935

The Abbey Gum Vendor is a nice-looking little machine, especially when its aluminum finish is buffed up like chrome. The customer slid his money into the cash tray and the machine delivered the product to the plate-like tray. The Abbey is very small in size, and it was designed for limited space locations.

POOR	FAIR	GOOD	EXCELLENT
$30	$45	$60	$75

Adam's Gum Vendor
circa 1945

Adam's Gum Company was an old hand at the business of vending gum. This is one of their innovations for selling gum. A multiple row concept much like cigarettes, gave the customer a great deal of choice, with 6 different selections.

POOR	FAIR	GOOD	EXCELLENT
$60	$80	$100	$125

Advance 1¢ Matches
1915

Advance displayed their matches with a beautiful glass dome. The base was cast iron with ornate little feet. It's amazing how something as simple as a match vendor could be made to look so classy.

POOR	FAIR	GOOD	EXCELLENT
$250	$330	$410	$500

Advance Gumball
1923

Advance manufacturing of Chicago, Illinois, had reasonable success with their simple reliable machines. Metal base parts were tin and the front plate was nickel over brass. They came painted in a variety of bright colors. However, red was the most popular, as was the case with many of the other manufacturers.

POOR	FAIR	GOOD	EXCELLENT
$100	$130	$160	$200

Appleton Gumball
circa 1920

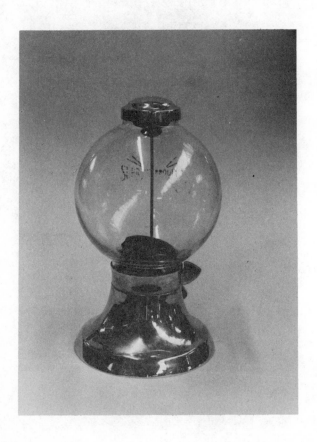

This machine features solid brass construction with a shiny nickel plate over the top. Appletons were produced in Cedar Rapids, Iowa, and looked pretty much the same from model to model.

POOR	FAIR	GOOD	EXCELLENT
$125	$165	$205	$250

Climax
1920

This cast iron based Climax has very nice lines. Climax is noted for its unique machines. This model shows a transition from the earlier, more ornate machines, to the more streamline styling. This was the last Climax produced.

POOR	FAIR	GOOD	EXCELLENT
$250	$350	$450	$550

Columbus "B"
circa 1920

This Columbus bulk vendor features the round globe, and the bell bottom base. One of the most common of the Columbus machines, because they were produced in large numbers. Note the original decal, and the embossed Columbus star on the globe. Early models were cast iron, and later models were cast aluminum.

POOR	FAIR	GOOD	EXCELLENT
$90	$120	$150	$175

Columbus "B" Bulk Vendor
with slug ejector
circa 1920

The most unusual feature of this Columbus model "B" is its add-on slug ejector. These could be specially ordered from the company. Slug ejectors were seldom used, and it can be assumed that this machine probably came from a location with undesirable clientele.

POOR	FAIR	GOOD	EXCELLENT
$100	$140	$180	$225

Columbus "B" Bulk Vendor
circa 1935

Columbus manufactured a huge variety of gumball and bulk vending machines. The one pictured is a Bell Bottom bulk vendor with a hex globe. Note the original barrel locks; they are important to the value of the machine. Original decals are also a big plus feature.

POOR	FAIR	GOOD	EXCELLENT
$75	$100	$125	$150

Columbus Model 21
circa 1920

This Columbus features a somewhat different base design that most of the other Columbus machines. The model shown includes the Columbus star hexagonal globe, and original barrel locks.

POOR	FAIR	GOOD	EXCELLENT
$100	$135	$170	$200

Columbus "A"
circa 1920

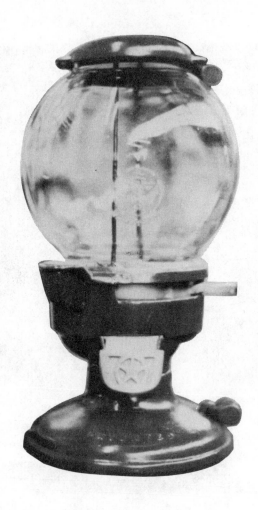

This Columbus hourglass cast iron base is definitely recognized as a classic. Fortunately they were produced in large enough number that prices are not exorbitant. Note the embossed Columbus star on the globe and the Columbus barrel locks.

POOR	FAIR	GOOD	EXCELLENT
$135	$180	$225	$275

Columbus Bimore Double Vendor
circa 1925

Double vendors started to get popular in the 1920's. The idea of course, was to give the customer more choices. This Columbus was porcelain over cast iron. it vended ball gum on one side, and any bulk product, such as peanuts, on the other.

POOR	FAIR	GOOD	EXCELLENT
$200	$275	$325	$400

Diamond Book Matches
circa 1920

One penny and a turn of the dial gave the customer 1 to 4 packs of book matches. The merchant had the option of setting the vendor to deliver 1 to 4 books. Notice the window in the upper left corner that was changeable to announce how many books were being vended.

POOR	FAIR	GOOD	EXCELLENT
$225	$320	$375	$450

Doremus Cigar Vendor
circa 1907

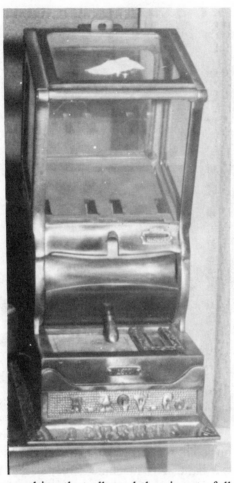

A very simple machine that allowed the cigar to fall into the tray because of its slanted top. A coin released the lever and allowed the customer to receive his purchase.

with cigar cutter

POOR	FAIR	GOOD	EXCELLENT
$1,000	$1,300	$1,600	$2,000

without cigar cutter

$750	$1,000	$1,250	$1,500

Smilin' Sam
1931 (1975)

Smilin' Sam was first brought out in 1931, and later reproduced in 1975. Insert your coin, pull his tongue, and he drops a measure of peanuts into your hand. This machine is very similar to the Happy Jap in concept, so it's very likely that it was a case of one company borrowing another's idea.

1931

POOR	FAIR	GOOD	EXCELLENT
$450	$600	$750	$900

1975

POOR	FAIR	GOOD	EXCELLENT
$150	$200	$250	$300

Hawkeye
circa 1931

Hawkeye featured a 6-sided cast aluminum base, usually painted in bright red. The gate, and the coin mechanisms were polished aluminum, which helped to dress up the machine.

POOR	FAIR	GOOD	EXCELLENT
$75	$100	$125	$150

International Vending
Match Machine
circa 1910

The cylinder revolved within the glass dome and dropped a box of matches into the chute. Part of the fun in buying these matches was to watch the machine work.

POOR	FAIR	GOOD	EXCELLENT
$600	$800	$1,000	$1,250

The Vendor
circa 1930

The cast iron base on this model was standard, and jobbers changed the top around to fit their needs. It's interesting how the variety of globes could change the entire look of a machine. Notice the primitive look of the Mason jar shape globe shown.

POOR	FAIR	GOOD	EXCELLENT
$60	$80	$100	$125

Victor Model V
circa 1940

Victor represents the no nonsense, boxey shapes of the 1940's. These were good working, inexpensive machines, and they were produced in large numbers. The original decal on the machine pictured adds to the value of the machine.

POOR	FAIR	GOOD	EXCELLENT
$40	$55	$70	$85

Victor "Baby Grand"
circa 1940

The Baby Grand was produced in a variety of models, including card vendor, jawbreaker, novelty, bulk, and gumball models. The sides were varnished oak, and that added a nice touch. Unfortunately the viewing portions are made of plastic, instead of glass.

POOR	FAIR	GOOD	EXCELLENT
$30	$40	$50	$65

White
Happy Jap
1902

For 1¢ the happy Jap would show a gum through his mouth to the awaiting customer. This was accomplished by a small clockwork motor mechanism. The machine was made of cast iron, and painted in vivid colors.

POOR	FAIR	GOOD	EXCELLENT
$800	$1,060	$1,320	$1,600

Zeno
circa 1895

Zeno machines were always a little unusual. For example, this machine offered the following flavors: Pineapple, yucca, licorice, peppermint, lemonade, vanilla cream, and pepsin. There was no choice, however; once the penny was inserted a clock mechanism pushed the gum out of the column and it fell down a chute into the hands of the customer.

POOR	FAIR	GOOD	EXCELLENT
$325	$425	$525	$650

Simmons Model A
circa 1930

This Simmons instructed the customer in a 1-2-3 sequence on the front casting. Number 1, insert coin, number 2, push lever, number 3, turn knob. If the buyer wasn't tired after all that, he could open the goods door, and receive the merchandise. Notice the geometric designs in the globe, and the porcelain finish.

POOR	FAIR	GOOD	EXCELLENT
$85	$115	$150	$175

Star Gum Vendor
circa 1935

The Star Gum Vendor has an interesting shape, with its triangular hexagonal globe. Star Quality Gum was advertised to have flavor all through. Whether or not this was a false advertising claim is hard to say. It probably was, however, since false advertising claims were common in early sales promotions.

POOR	FAIR	GOOD	EXCELLENT
$75	$100	$125	$150

Tom Thumb
circa 1920

Miniature gumball machines would never make it today because of theft problems. However, in the good old days, this little guy was great for the location with limited counter space.

POOR	FAIR	GOOD	EXCELLENT
$65	$85	$105	$125

Several manufacturers came out with tray style vendors for the customer that were clumsy. This way, the product could be scooped up from the immaculately clean tray, if spilled. The machine was made of aluminum, and painted in two tones.

POOR	FAIR	GOOD	EXCELLENT
$60	$80	$100	$125

**Ford "Chrome"
circa 1950**

The Ford Chrome is familiar to almost everyone who has ever purchased a gumball. Many of these machines are still on location, however, most have been converted to plastic globes. Because of their great numbers and late vintage, they are very available and fairly inexpensive.

POOR	FAIR	GOOD	EXCELLENT
$30	$40	$50	$60

**Lawrence Double
Bulk Vendor
circa 1940**

This trim little aluminum bulk vendor very efficiently handled the sale of nuts and candies.

POOR	FAIR	GOOD	EXCELLENT
$50	$65	$80	$100

C. E. Leebold
circa 1920

Leebold was noted for its huge globes that held a lot of product. This made the operator happy, since it meant fewer refills. The base was made of cast aluminum. Note that the marquee is missing on this model.

POOR	FAIR	GOOD	EXCELLENT
$90	$120	$150	$185

The Leebold
circa 1920

The beautiful Leebold looks older than it is because of its beautiful Victorian styling which had a revival in the 20's. One telltale sign of its age is the fact that it is made of cast aluminum. Unfortunately they are quite rare and few are to be seen around. What else can be said, it's a classic.

POOR	FAIR	GOOD	EXCELLENT
$700	$930	$1,160	$1,400

Log Cabin Duplex Vendor
circa 1927

Giving the customer two choices brought more money to the operators. Log Cabin was made of aluminum, and it was polished to catch a potential buyer's attention. Notice the very modular modern lines that was an unusual style for the 1920's.

POOR	FAIR	GOOD	EXCELLENT
$70	$90	$110	$145

Mansfield Automatic Clerk
1901

The Automatic Clerk is a handsome machine with an etched front glass. It was unique in that the clock wound mechanism was completely visible to the customer. A penny would set the escalator in motion, flipping the gum over the top of the column, and ringing a bell.

POOR	FAIR	GOOD	EXCELLENT
$250	$330	$410	$500

Master Fantail 1¢/5¢
1931

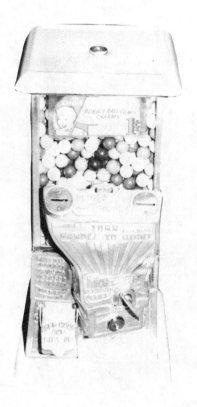

Master Fantail is a classic that is sought after by collectors. A customer could deposit a penny in one slot, or a nickel in another, and receive varied amounts of the product. The finish was porcelain, and it came in several different colors. Note that the patent date on all Master machines says 1923; but they weren't actually distributed until 1930.

POOR	FAIR	GOOD	EXCELLENT
$200	$300	$400	$500

Master 1¢/5¢
1931

The Master 1¢/5¢ is not to be confused with the more valuable Master 1¢/5¢ fantail. With this machine the penny and nickel were both inserted in the same slot. A penny received one measure, and a nickel received a little more than 5 times that amount. The top and bottom of the machine were made of porcelain for extra durability.

POOR	FAIR	GOOD	EXCELLENT
$100	$150	$175	$225

Master 1¢
1931

Norris manufacturing made a name for themselves with the Master gumball and bulk vendors of the style pictured. The top and base were finished in a bright porcelain, usually black, green, or white. The square globe design was a plus in that if it was broken it was easily replaced with a piece of standard glass.

POOR	FAIR	GOOD	EXCELLENT
$75	$100	$125	$150

Mutoscope
Old Mill
1928

International mutoscope, famous for their flip card machines, also produced the Old Mill. For a mere penny, the customer got a scoop full of candy, gum, or whatever. Because of the random nature of the scoop, the customer experienced a mild sensation of gambling. The unusual graphics are especially noteworthy on this machine.

POOR	FAIR	GOOD	EXCELLENT
$425	$565	$705	$850

National Vending
Colgan's Gum
circa 1902

Taffy tolu had to be an interesting gum flavor. These rare machines gave 1 stick for a penny. As an extra inducement, 2 sticks were given for every 5th penny.

POOR	FAIR	GOOD	EXCELLENT
$900	$1,200	$1,500	$1,800

Northwestern Merchandiser 31
1931

Northwestern put porcelain on most of their machines. The reason of course was to have a durable and attractive finish. This merchandiser is cast iron, with a blue and yellow porcelain finish. Note the original Northwestern decal.

POOR	FAIR	GOOD	EXCELLENT
$75	$100	$125	$150

Northwestern "33"
1933

Porcelain finishes were used on all of the early Northwestern machines. This finish was durable and held up to the hard knocks of being on location. Many examples of the Northwesterns have survived with their original porcelain, thus giving the modern-day collector a shot at having a machine with an all-original finish.

POOR	FAIR	GOOD	EXCELLENT
$75	$100	$125	$150

Northwestern 33
1933

Northwestern used a logical approach for model numbers, since they were simply the year of production. This model was porcelain (usually bright red) over cast iron. Note the original decal inviting the customer to "try some."

POOR	FAIR	GOOD	EXCELLENT
$75	$100	$125	$150

Northwestern Vendor
circa 1950

Like most of the other gumball manufacturers, Northwestern updated their machines in later years. Notice the very modular design
with the shiny chrome finish. The viewing area also made use of
plastic, instead of glass.

POOR	FAIR	GOOD	EXCELLENT
$25	$30	$40	$55

Oak Acorn
circa 1950

Almost any kid who has ever purchased a gumball, or bulk-vend candy will recognize the acorn symbol. Oak Mfg. was king of the gumball vendors in the 40's and 50's and beyond. Their symbol can still be seen on gumball machines across the country.

POOR	FAIR	GOOD	EXCELLENT
$35	$45	$55	$65

Oronite Lighter Fluid Dispenser
circa 1930

Notice the resemblance to an early gas pump? For 1¢ the customer was treated to a fillup for his lighter. Why don't we see these vendors anymore? One reason could be that their diminutive size opens up all kinds of theft possibilities.

POOR	FAIR	GOOD	EXCELLENT
$135	$180	$225	$275

Postage Vendor
circa 1910

Postage stamps were a natural for vending machines; everyone hates to run to the post office just for stamps. This early model has a cast iron base and top. Notice the great use of beveled glass for displaying the stamps and mechanism.

POOR	FAIR	GOOD	EXCELLENT
$200	$260	$320	$400

Premiere Card Vendor
circa 1950

The Premiere vended the customer both a ball gum, and a personality card. Personality cards were big in the 1950's, and many kids were hooked on collecting sets. Interestingly enough, some of these sets of cards are beginning to have value today.

POOR	FAIR	GOOD	EXCELLENT
$40	$55	$70	$85

Price Collar Button Vendor
1901

Little columns of collar buttons displayed the wares for this machine. Much like a modern vendor, the customer selected the style he wanted by moving the selector wheel. For those people out there who don't have the faintest idea what a collar button is, they were used to attach removable collars to gentlemen's shirts.

POOR	FAIR	GOOD	EXCELLENT
$475	$625	$775	$950

Pulver
circa 1931

Pulver vendors were produced for many years, and it's easy to understand why. Kids as well as adults love to put their money in and watch them go. After inserting a penny, a clock movement set a figural character into motion, and a stick of gum would drop into the tray.

POOR	FAIR	GOOD	EXCELLENT
$175	$225	$275	$350

Regal gumball vendor
circa 1935

Modular design and a teardrop globe identify the Regal vendor. This model was aluminum, as was the case with most gumball machines produced in the late 1930's.

POOR	FAIR	GOOD	EXCELLENT
$45	$60	$75	$90

Regal Candy Machine
circa 1935

Regal machines are easily identifiable because of the straight-lined, modular base. This model vends jawbreakers for a nickel.

POOR	FAIR	GOOD	EXCELLENT
$45	$60	$75	$90

Regal Hot Nut Vendor
circa 1950

The special attraction with this vendor was its function of vending hot nuts. A light bulb served to keep the nuts warm, and attract the attention of passersby. This is an interesting machine that's a little different from the run of the mill vendors. A glass light cover indicated the machine was made in the 1930's, and a plastic cover indicates the 1950's.

Plastic

POOR	FAIR	GOOD	EXCELLENT
$30	$45	$60	$75

Glass

$75	$100	$125	$150

302

Zeno Gum
circa 1910

Decorated in bright yellow porcelain, the Zeno was an attention getting machine. After a penny was dropped into the slot, a clockwork
mechanism pushed the gum over the top of the column, and into
the product tray. A small viewing window reassured the customer
that there was gum in the machine.

POOR	FAIR	GOOD	EXCELLENT
$200	$260	$320	$400

BIBLIOGRAPHY AND DEALER SECTION

Books

Antique Slot Machines by Richard and Barbara Reddock, Wallace Homestead Book Co., 1912 Grand Ave., Des Moines, Iowa 50209.

Coin Slot Guides by Richard M. Bueschel. A series of in depth guides on various machines. Coin Slot, P.O. Box 176, Luzerne, PA 18709 Co. 80033.

Collector's Treasury of Antique Slot Machines from Contemporary Advertising. Edited by Peter Bach, Port Era Books, Arcadia, Ca. 91006.

Drop Coin Here by Ken Rubin, Crown Publishing, One Park Avenue, New York, N.Y. 10016.

Encyclopedia of Automatic Musical Instruments by Q. David Bowers, Vestal Press,, Box 97, Vestal, New York, 13850

Gumball Machines Right or Wrong by Abraham Van der Vliet, edited and arranged by Philip and Julie Cunningham. Published by Mead Publishing Corporatiion, 21176 South Alameda St., Long Beach, Ca. 90810

An Illustrated Price Guide to the 100 Most Collectible Trade Stimulators by Richard M. Bueschel. See Coin Slot, P. O. Box 176, Luzerne, PA 18709.

An Illustrated Guide to the 100 Most Collectible Slot Machines, by Richard M. Bueschel. See above.

An Illustrated Price Guide to the 100 Most Collectible Slot Machines, volume 2, by Richard M. Bueschel. See above.

An Illustrated Price Guide to the 100 Most Collectible Slot Machines, volume 3, by Richard M. Bueschel. See above.

Jukebox Saturday Night by J. Kirvine, available from Jukebox Collector 2545, S.C. 60th St. Des Moines, Iowa, 50317, or John Kirvine, 102 Raleigh House, Dolphine Square, London SWI

Jukebox, The Golden Age by Vincent Lynch and Bill Henkin, Lancaster-Miller, 3165 Adeline St., Berkebley, Ca.

The Official Loose Change Blue Book of Antique Slot Machines, by Stan and Betty Wilker, The Mead Company, 21176 South Alameda St., Long Beach, Ca. 90180

The Official Loose Change Red Book of Antique Trade Stimulators and Counter Games, by Stan and Betty Wilker, The Mead Company, 21176 South Alameda St., Long Beach, Ca. 90810

Owner's Pictorial Guide for the Care and Understanding of the Mills Bell Slot Machine, by Robert N. Geddes and Daniel R. Mead, The Mead Company, 21176 South Alameda St., Long Beach, California 90810

Owner's Pictorial Guide for Care and Understanding of the Jennings Bell Slot Machine by Robert N. Geddes and Daniel R. Mead, The Mead Company, 21176 South Alameda St., Long Beach, 90810

Owner's Pictorial Guide for the Care and Understanding of the Watling Bell Slot Machine, by Robert N. Geddes and Daniel R. Mead, The Mead Company, 21176 South Alameda St., Long Beach, Ca. 90810

Pinball Portfolio, by Harry McKeown, Chartwell Books, 110 Enterprise Avenue, Secaucus, New Jersey 070094

Slot Machines on Parade, by Robert N. Geddes and Daniel R. Mead, The Mead Company 21176 South Alameda St., Long Beach, California 90810

Slot Machines, A Pictorial Review, by David G. Christensen The Vestal Press, Box 97, Vestal, New York 13850

Tilt The Pinball Book, Home Maintenance, by Candace Ford Tolbert and Jim Alan Tolbert, Creative Arts Book Company, 833 Bancroft Way, Berkeley, Ca. 94710

Catalogues; with parts, literature of machines listed for sale:

"Antique Slot Machine Part Company", catalogue of reproduction slot machine parts, Tom Kahl, 238 Hecker Dr., Dundee, Il. 60118, (312) 428-8476

"Antique Aparatus" Catalogue of replacement parts for Wurlitzer jukeboxes, 13355 Ventura Blvd., Sherman Oaks, Ca., 91423 (213) 995-1169

Chicago Antique Slot Machine So., catalogue of reproduction slot machine parts, 1778 W. Algonquin Rd., Arlington Hts., Id. 60005, (302) 392-2212

Coin Slot Library List: books, old catalog reprints, posters, service manuals on antique coin-operated machines. The Coin Slot, P.O. Box 612, Wheatridge, Colorado 80033

East Coast Casino Antiques Catalogue: very nice, illustrated booklet of primarily gambling paraphernalia with some coin-operated gambling devices; East Coast Casino Antiques, 98 Main St., Fishkill, New York 12524

Evans and Frink, list of reprints: reelstrips, paycards, decals, instruction sheets, and mint wrappers for slot machines and trade stimulators, 7999 Keller Road, Cincinnati, Ohio 45243

Jukebox Junction: illustrated catalogue of reproduction jukebox parts and literature with related items; Juekbox Junction, Box 1081, Des Moines, Iowa 50311

Mechanical Music Center, Inc., 25 Kings Hwy. North, Box 88, Darien, Conn. 06830; very nice illustrated catalogue of musical instruments (some coin-ops)

Michael's Vintage Games, catalogue of reproduction slot machine parts, 623 North Main St., Mount Prospect, Ill., 60056 (312) 398-7633

Mr. Russell; long list of books dealing with coin-operated antiques; 2404 West 111th St., Chicago, Ill. 60655

Slot Dynasty; list of reelstrips and paycards for trade stimulators; (415) 756-1189

Specialty Slots Corp. Catalogue of Watling replacement parts. Clybourn Ave., P.O. Box 1426, Sun Valley, Ca. 91352 (213) 765-1210, (213) 877-1664

TAJ Distributing, 621 Miller St., Lucerne Pa. 18709. Large supply of books and literature related to coin-operated.

Vestal Press Catalogue; illustrated catalogue of books on antiques, with some on coin-operated antiques; The Vestal Press, Box 97, Vestal, New York 13850

Dealers:

These either buy, sell, restore, or sell restoration parts for antique coin-operated machines.

Please remember that I am not endorsing any of the following dealers. This list is designed to inform the reader. I will apologize for any dealers I have left out. If you would like to be included in future editions, just send a business card addressed to: Jerry Ayliffe, P.O. Box El Dorado Hills, Ca. 95630. As an afterthought, I will include myself in this illustrious list. I buy, sell, trade and restore coin-operated antiques. I can be reached at the address above, or at (916) 933-0952

California

Antique Apparatus, Co., 13355 Ventura Blvd., Sherman Oaks, Ca. 91423, (213) 995-1169, Wurlitzer replacement parts

Antique Jukebox Company, 2222 East Washington Blvd., Los Angeles, Cal. 90021 (213) 589-5903. Specializes in repair and restoration parts for antique jukes, and antique jukeboxes for sale.

Authenic Antique Slots, Dennis B. Salenti, P.O. Box 986, Mt. Shasta, Ca. 96067 (916) 926-4126, sales and restoration.

Baker Lady Luck Emporium,, P.O. Box 4117, Wildside, Ca. 94]62 (415) 851-7188. Antique slot machines and old west collectibles.

Bruce Benjamin, Palo Alto, (415) 328-6006, buys and sells coin-operated antiques and related items.

Brooks Novelty Antiques, 885-57th St., Sacramento, Ca. 95819 (916) 457-6806. Coin-operated sales, repair, and restoration.

Bill Butterfield, Dixon. (916) 678-3435. Buys, sells, restores, jukeboxes.

The Classic Jukebox Co., P.O. Box 1296, Reseda, Ca. 91335 (213) 886-3725. Wurlitzer parts and paraphernalia.

Tom Cockrill, 4430 Coliseum Wy., Oakland, Ca. 94601 (415) 536-3344, specializes in arcade.

Phil Cunningham, Burbank, Ca. 91505, (213) 845-4964, specializes in gum and peanut machines, especially Columbus.

Fallentich Ent., 9571 Garden Grove Blvd., Garden Grove, Ca. 92644, (714) 537-7568, buys, sells, trades, repairs, and restores, slot machines.

Free Play, 35 East St. Joseph St., Arcadia, Ca. 91006, (213) 445-5710. All kinds of coin-operated machines bought and sold.

Tony Goodstone, P.O. Box 35683, Los Angeles, Ca. 90035 (213) 857-1307. Specializes in all facets of restoration work including artwork, special painting and finishing effects, specialty glasswork, etc.

Dick Graves, Oakland, (415) 835-1366, buys and sells pinball and arcade.

The Gumball Magnate, D.R. Williams, Box 758, Kentfield, Ca. 94904, (415) 435-4089. Buys, sells, and trades all coin-ops, especially gumball and nut machines.

Johnson's Antiques and Things, 1767 Church, San Francisco, Ca. 94131, (415) 282-8102, (415) 282-8102, (415) 824-2942. Specializes in coin-operated antiques and unusual Americana.

Judith's Jukes, 827 Folsom St., San Francisco, (415) 777-2930, buy, sell, and restore classic jukeboxes.

John Kehlet, Sacramento, Ca. 93821 (916) 487-3356, (916) 726-3233. Slot repair, restorations, sales.

Memory Lane, 11490 Burbank Blvd., No. Hollywood, Ca. 91601 (213) 985-7640. Coin-operated antiques, bought, sold, and restored.

Meyers Novelty Antiques, Bud Meyer, (415) 537-5744, (415) 582-8039. Buy, sell, trade, slot machines and arcade games.

Musee Mecanique, The Cliff House, San Francisco, Ca. (415) 621-7400. No machines for sale, but you can play some old arcade machines for pocket change.

Newhall Pharmacy, 24275 San Fernando Rd., NewHall, Ca. 91321 (305) 259-1311, Buy, sell, trade, repair, and restore coin-operated and related items.

Morry O'Connell, P.O. Box 1, Mt. Eden, Ca. 94557, (415) 785-0657 antique slot machines and parts, buy, sell, and trade.

Neil Rasmussen's Antique Designs, 755 Loma Verde Ave., Pal Alto, (415) 493-5552, offering coin-operated and related items for sale or lease.

Slot Dynasty, Daly City, Ca. 94015, (415) 756-1189. Award cards, and reelstrips for trade stimulators, also restorations; buys trade stimulators.

Specialty Slot Corporation, 7506 Clybourn Ave., P.O. Box 1426, Sun Valley, Ca. 91352 (213) 877-1664. Specializes in manufactured Mills and Watling slot parts, catalogue available.

Squires and Corrie, 373 South Claremont, San Mateo, Ca. 94401 (415) 342-6737. Slot sales and restoration.

Summit Fabrications, 18247 Bayview Drive, Los Gatos, Ca. 95030 (408) 353-2619. Antique jukebox sales and restoration.

Superior Slots, Jim and Susan Landon, Sunnyvale, Ca. (408) 245-3514. Buy and sell slots.

Warren's Antiques, 1558 A St., Castro Valley, Ca. 94546 (415) 582-7446, 582-8927. All types of coin-operated and related items.

D.R. Williams, Box 758, Kentfield, Ca. 94904 (415) 435-4089. Buy, sell, gumball and peanut vending machines.

Florida

One Arm Bandit, 1182 N. State Road 7, Ft. Lauderdale, Fl., 33313, (305) 792-GAME. Buy, sell, and repair slots and jukeboxes.

Miami Antique Slot Machine Company, 13738 Biscayne Blvd., North Miami, Fl., 33181, (305) 947-9207. Coin-operated sales and restoration.

Illinois

Amusement Rarities, 5559 Blackstone, Chicago, 60637, (312) 7526263, buy, sell, gambling, arcade and vending.

Antique Games, Ltd., 2728 Dundee Rd., Northbrook, Il., 60062 (312) 272-2270. Slot machine, and video games.

Antique Slot Machine Part Co., 238 Hecker Dr., Dundee, Il., 60118 (312) 428-8476. Reproduction slot machine parts.

Bandits, 458 Central Ave., Highland Park, Ill. 60035 (312) 433-2578. Coin-operated and gambling equipment.

Bernie Berten, 9420 S. Turnball Ave. Evergreen Park, Ill., 60642 (312) 499-0688 Slot machine springs and parts.

Chicago Antique Slot Machine Co., Arlington Heights, Ill. 60005, (312) 392-2212. Slot-related repair, restoration, and sales. Also carry reel strips, cash boxes, award cards, locks, etc.

Coin-Op Amusements, Steve Gronowski, 8008 Memory Lane, Chicago, Ill., 60656 (312) 775-4023, coin-operated machines for sale.

Pete Hansen's Antique Slot Machine Co., 9682 Reding Circle, Des Plaines, Il. 60016 (312) 299-6213. Sales, Serivce, parts, restoration.

Home Arcade Corporation, 1108 Front St., Lisle, Il. 60532, (312) 964-2555, coin-operated machines sold and serviced.

J and R Saloon Novelties, Russ Newman, 819 Meadow Drive, RR 2, Elgin, Il., 70120 (312) 464-5661. Coin-operated antiques for sale.

Marshall Larks, Skokie, (312) 679-4765. Buy, sell, gumball and peanut vending machines.

Michael's Vintage Games, 623 N. Main St., Mount Prospect, Il. 60056 (312) 398-7633. Specializes in Mills reproduction cabinets.

Allan Pall, (312) 771-7446, Chicago. Specializes in rare coin-operated machines.

Penny Lane Antiques, 4820 N. Troy, Chicago, Il., 70625, (312) 478-3535. Coin-operated antiques, especially jukeboxes and slots bought and sold.

Mr. Russell, 2404 W. 111th St. Chicago, Il. 60655 (312) 233-3205, carries every book in print related to coin-operated machines; lists available.

The Slot Doctor, 239 E. Main St., Cary, Il. 60013, (312) 639-SLOT. Slot machine restorations.

Maryland

Bodzer's Antique Slot Machine Company, 2300 Perry Hall Blvd. Baltimore, Maryland, (301) 256-0062. Antique Slot sales.

Home Amusement Co., 11910 Parklawn Drive, Rockville, Md., 20852 (301) 468-0070. Buy, sell, repair and restore coin-ops.

Massachusetts

Rick Lee, Box 105, Lincoln, Mass. 01773, (617) 259-0807. Buys, sells, repairs antique coin-operated and related.

Michigan

Jay Mihelich Co., 1622 Mills Ave., No. Muskegon, Mi., 49445, (616) 744-9214, slot machines and jukeboxes.

Missouri

St. Louis Slot Machine Company, 2111 S. Brentwood Blvd., St. Louis, Missouri 63144, (314) 961-4612, antique coin-operated machines and parts.

Montana

Tony Trading Post, 209 East Park St., Butte, Montana 59701 (406) 723-0924, buy, sale, and trade if operated by a coin.

Nevada

A and P Slots, 350 N. Virginia, Reno, Nevada, 89501 (702) 322-0662. Slot machines; buy, sell, trade, repair and restoration.

The Antique Gambler, 3443 Industrial Road, Las Vegas, Nevada 89103, (702) 369-0743, sell and trade antique slot machines, also repairs and restoration.

Victorian Casino Antiques, 1421 South Main St., Las Vegas, Nev., 89104, (702) 382-2466. Specializing in large auctions with desirable antique coin-operated antiques and related items.

New York

Casino Antiques, 2956 Merrick Road, Bellmore, New York 11710, (516) 783-8300, custom made, ornate cast iron slot machine stands.

East Coast Casino Antiques, 98 Main St., Fishkill, N.Y. 12524, (914) 896-9492, specializes in antique gambling paraphernalia and some coin-operated equipment, large selection of literature available.

Ohio

Evans and Frink, 7999 Keller Road, Cincinnati, Ohio 45243. Slot machine reel strips and award cards; catalogue available.

Mike Gorski, 1770 Dover Center Road, Westlake, Ohio 44145, (216) 871-6071; antique slot machines, penny arcade, bought, sold, traded.

Hoke, Inc., 7038 Hoke Rd., Clayton, Ohio 45315, (513) 836-3101, (513) 836-2018. Buy, sell, and restore antique coin-operated.

Ed Kravita, 220 Brydon Rd., Kettring, Ohio 45419 (513) 298-2370, gumball, slot, coin-op machines, sell, buy, and trade

South Dakota

Cummings Enterprises, Inc., 300 S. Lewis, Sioux Falls, S.D. 57103, (605) 336-3399, (605) 336-3398 (answering service), buy, sell, and trade coin-operated machines.

Washington

Craig Willardson, P.O. Box 8296, Spokane, Wa., 99203, (509) 747-2609. Restoration and repair of antique slot machines.

Periodicals

"The Antique Trader", weekly tabloid, misc. antique classifieds. The Antique Trader, Box 1050, Dubuque, Iowa

"The Coin Slot", monthly magazine, coin-operated antiques, articles and classified ads, The Coin Slot, P.O. Box 176, Luzerne, PA 18709.

"The Jukebox Collector" monthly newsletter, jukebox ads and articles. 2545 S.E. 60th St., Des Moines, Iowa 50317.

"Loose Change", monthly magazine, coin-operated antiques, articles and classified ads, Mead Company, 21176 South Alameda St., Long Beach, California 90810

"Nickel A Tune" magazine with articles on jukeboxes and classified ads. 9514-9 Reseda Blvd., Space 613, Northridge, Ca. 91324, (213) 701-1221